CONCILIUM

Religion in the Seventies

CONCILIUM

Religion in the Seventies

THE UNIFYING ROLE
OF THE BISHOP

Edited by

Edward Schillebeeckx

Herder and Herder

1972
HERDER AND HERDER NEW YORK
232 Madison Avenue, New York 10016

CONTENTS

PART II
BULLETIN

PART III
DOCUMENTATION CONCILIUM

Editorial

THE Church has passed through a time of unity in uniformity
and is now entering a period of unity in pluriformity, during
which the "peace of the Church" is possible only by way of differences and conflicts. There is consequently an urgent need for
dogmatic theologians to consider the role of the bishops in the
Church: that is, the episcopate as the traditionally binding factor
in the living community of faith. The unity of the Church is
certainly based on an interaction between the actual content of
faith (the Church as the "body of the Lord" and the "temple of
the Holy Spirit", especially in the celebration of the Eucharist,
the sharing of the one "body of the Lord") and the historically developed, social forms in which that unity is expressed. Just as it
would be incorrect to base a theology on these social forms, which
have come about in the course of history, so would it be wrong
to draw *a priori* theological conclusions about the actual forms
that the Church's unity and peace ought to take. The models of
the Church's unity that we use are bound to change in the course
of history. In the light of its "eschatological proviso", the Church
is always bound, in any response to social forms of unity and
"communion", to take a critical attitude towards all previously
existing social models.

In this number of *Concilium*, an attempt is made to throw
some light on this theme of "the bishop and the unity of the
Church" mainly from two viewpoints: that of the warnings provided by the experience of the Church in the past, and that of
the relation between the Christian message and the world of

today. The social differences between the biblical, medieval and modern situations lead us to ask repeatedly how, here and now, we can establish the unity and peace of the Church in the Christian community under the leadership of the bishops.

At the deepest level, the Church's unity is determined by the unity of the apostolic faith (however various the biblical expression of that faith may be) and the celebration and profession of this in the Eucharist, the sacrament of the Church's unity. As the witness and the interpreter of this faith, and as the one called to lead in the celebration of the Eucharist, the bishop plays a special part in bringing about and preserving peace in the Church. He is the point of reference of the life of faith of his community, and the authentic interpreter of the evangelical faith present in that community in its concrete historical situation. If he criticizes some of the ways in which his community expresses itself, he usually does so by confronting that community's experience of God's word with its experience elsewhere and in the past. The best safeguard of the continuity of the Christian message is, in any case, the redemptive testimony of man's individual and collective liberation by God in Christ (C. Molari).

This fundamental view of the Church is also clarified in the light of Eastern Orthodox ecclesiology, and emphasis is placed above all on the collegial leadership of the bishop with his *presbyterium* or college of priests in the local church, which is the point of departure for every ecclesiology. What is the "Church" but first and foremost the local church in which the Eucharist is celebrated with the bishop presiding and his priests assisting? The "parishes" of the Church (without a bishop) are therefore joined together to form the unity of a diocesan episcopal church, which in turn enjoys communion and good relationships with other local churches and their leaders. In this way, the bishops and the college of bishops exist in the sign of the unity of the Church (G. Wagner).

Unity within the diocesan church, and peace between the various diocesan churches, do not, however, imply "uniformity". Three examples in this number show that it is still possible to learn from fortunate and less fortunate attempts in the history of the Church to find solutions to conflicts that have arisen within it. The problem in each of these cases is, essentially, whether it is right for a local church (even if it has the representative of Peter as its bishop) to impose its local practice on other local churches, and thus to enforce unity through uniformity. The conflict between Bishop Polycarp and Pope Anicetus was solved by applying the principle of the *regula pacis* and, for the sake of peace in the Church, the bishop and the Pope acknowledged the divergence of a practice in each other's churches, although the difference in practice did not lack a doctrinal background. Certain "dogmatic uncertainties", however, were allowed to continue to exist, as N. Brox says, because peace in the Church was regarded as more important. Again, the conflict between Rome and Carthage (Bishop Cyprian) shows how an ecclesiology that is abused in a "dictatorial" manner is bound to fail—A. Davids claims that history has proved that Cyprian was in the wrong in this case. Finally, L. Meulenberg discusses the conflicts of Gregory VII, who is even now symbolic of contradiction because he was compelled by circumstances to follow a policy of increasing centralization.

The term "local church" should not, however, be understood simply in the territorial sense; and this wider application of the term raises, especially nowadays, the problem of the so-called "basic communities" with their critical attitudes. Here, too, the function of the bishop to maintain order in the Church cannot be overlooked, but he is, of course, bound to play the part of the confidant who takes risks here, rather than that of the leader or the one who takes the initiative. H.-M. Legrand analyses the implications of this new phenomenon.

The collegial leadership of the local community is expressed in the relationship between the bishop and his college of priests, but the practice that has been current since the ninth century and the law that has been in force since the end of the sixteenth century, according to which priests have to make a promise, a vow or an oath of obedience to their bishop (at the time of their ordination as subdeacons), go back to a feudal social custom. Collegial collaboration between priests in conjunction with, and subject to, the guidance of their bishops was given an actual social form in a kind of feudal oath made by the priest to his "liege lord", the bishop. Clearly, non-theological structures play a part in the actual relationship between the priest and his bishop. The question therefore arises as to how a more democratic leadership can be brought about in the Church in a situation in which social relationships have changed to the extent that absolute power structures have either disappeared or are at least sharply criticized, without any disobedience to Christ, the one Lord of the Church, or any lack of fidelity towards the apostolic office. A. Müller's article deals with this.

The Church and its unity are situated "in history". The question at once arises: what are the aspects of the "business organization" of the Church's unity? A free consensus of opinion—which, despite all pluriformity, certainly forms the basis of all unity—can only be brought about within the Church in an open society such as ours, if the bishop actively encourages communication, dialogue and the dissemination of information, opposes all manipulation of dialogue, and allows every opinion to be expressed. In his article, R. Huysmans discusses how the demands of "business organization" are expressed in the Church in this way, and how these are able to give concrete form to the Church as *communio* in the world of today.

C. Molari, in his contribution, states that the new type of bishop has not been invented by theologians or bureaucrats, but will grow out of the renewed community of believers. This has prompted us to ask three bishops to write about the function of their own communities, and their own episcopal roles in those communities with regard to the world and the Church. Cardinals and bishops who have already expressed clear views in public have deliberately not been asked. The men who have written for this issue are rather bishops active "in the field"— L. Proaño, bishop of Riobamba in Ecuador, A. Fragoso, a bishop in Brazil, and the Episcopalian bishop of New York, P. Moore, Jr.

Information is given in three bulletins about the possibilities of conducting a consensus of opinion in the Church. F. Haarsma examines whether it is indeed possible in principle to obtain such a consensus in an empirical, scientific manner, for example, by means of sociological surveys. The delicacy of this whole question can be seen from an investigation of catechisms in German-speaking (F. J. Kötter), and in French-speaking (J. C. Dhôtel), countries.

The theologian who was invited to write a fundamental article about "conflicts in the Church"—a bishop's conflict (a) with his own community, (b) with his fellow bishops, (c) with other bishops at a synod or council, and (d) with the Pope—has not been able to submit his contribution in time because of illness. For this reason, I have tried to make up for this deficiency by including in the Documentation F. Haarsma's informative article about a local Dutch *ecclesia*. This *ecclesia*, despite its very free and critical attitude within the Dutch province, has none the less accepted a guiding commission appointed by the Dutch bishops, and is clearly anxious to preserve unity and peace in situations obviously charged with conflict.

E. Schillebeeckx

PART I
ARTICLES

Carlo Molari

The Bishops' Witness to Apostolic Faith

IF ONE speaks of the crisis of the priestly identity, one thinks in-
stinctively of ordinary pastors. But perhaps it would be better to
consider the situation of the bishops. How often does one meet
bishops who feel rather at a loss. Many of them think of themselves as bureaucrats, dedicated to solemn ceremonial and official-
dom. Others suffer from a serious isolation in their present calling, separated from the people and perhaps even more from the
clergy. The majority of them are firmly attached (necessarily so
by the nature of things) to the traditional functions bound up
with the presence of the bishop in urban centres. There is the
solemn character of the episcopacy, the outward dignity, the
familiar clichés. And this is not because of any ill will. Often it
corresponds to the wishes of the clergy and of the people. It may
be that the few bishops who try to free themselves from this
situation feel more isolated than the rest; they are misunderstood
by their brother bishops and at times meet with difficulties in
their relations with the faithful. Misunderstood by their own
brethren, living in isolation from, and at times under suspicion
by, the central authorities, many bishops admit to extraordinary
difficulties in fulfilling their mission, and often are unable to
grasp its real meaning. "What can we do?" they ask; and "What
ought we to do?" There have been occasions, met with more
or less everywhere, when it has been shown how pressing is the
question of finding a new "image" for the bishop.

The means of doing this is not at all easy, but the process has begun. It is no problem to find a new "image" for the priest, and it may be that it is not so very difficult for the bishop.

These preliminary reflections explain the reasons for and the scope of the following notes. They are not an historical analysis, not a piece of biblical research. They are only suggestions about some of the features possessed by a witness to the faith, drawn from the experience of our own time.

I. The Witness of Freedom

This affirmation of the bishops' witness to the faith of the apostles is no new thing and is not intended to justify changes in the traditional conception of the episcopal mission. But what is changed is perhaps the way of understanding the faith and its apostolic character. I accept the fact, the values and the theological basis of this apostleship. My purpose is to clarify its significance. The Christian message was presented from the beginning as a witness, a witness to the fact that Christ is living, having passed through death, and that his spirit has power to give freedom to all who receive it in faith. These two aspects are closely related; the one is inconceivable without the other. It is not possible to proclaim that Christ has risen and at the same time not to affirm that he is the "living spirit" (1 Cor. 15. 43). This is the starting-point of man's thorough self-renewal. But this affirmation is impossible, and inefficacious, if man does not experience his own transformation, if, that is to say, he does not receive that liberating power that comes from the risen Christ. Because of this, the proclamation of the Resurrection must be accompanied by the "manifestation of the Spirit and its power" (1 Cor. 2. 24): the power of God, that is, to free us from sin, causing us to embrace a new way of life.

Accordingly, witness has as its object neither an intellectual affirmation nor a situation that has ended, but an actual reality which transforms those who believe in the operative power of Christ alive in God.

If the witness concerned nothing but a past event and could be reduced definitely to an intellectual statement, there would be no need of witnesses. It would be sufficient to have testimonies recorded in documents. All one would need would be a monument or a commemorative tablet to hand down to posterity what had occurred. But, since the apostolic witness is related to the present age, it is not enough to have testimonies; one has to have witnesses, that is, living persons. The proclamations of the apostles and all their successors concern human existence, and this acquires significance only in so far as it is related to the efficacy of its influence on life. It is a declaration of freedom and salvation to the end that every man, every day, can begin a new life, can find new ways of living with his brethren, and can surmount the barriers of egotism and hatred so that, realizing a profound reality of common consciousness, he can overcome the limitations of his own existence until he reaches the extremity of the bounds set by his individual nature and by death. Those who have not experienced renewal cannot know what they should proclaim; those who are ignorant of the existence of the sons of God do not know what kind of freedom they should proclaim. In other words, the witness the Church has to bear before the world means a state of life which becomes aware of itself only in the moment in which it comes into actual existence.

The proclamation of liberty (that is, of salvation) can accordingly only be made by those who come to realize their own renewal. The apostles began to preach when they discovered that they had, as it were, been "turned upside down", when they could display to the crowds the works of the Spirit, "which you see and hear" (Acts 2. 33).

In this way, they preached salvation to men, and called upon them to hope—to rid themselves of anguish about their future, in the certainty that a really new day would open tomorrow, when they would receive the gift of God. This truth is so great that it has not yet completely entered into the communal structures of men's existence; for this they must look to the future. To wait for this is not a mere expectation of something that has not yet occurred, but the acceptance, in a new and richer manner, of the gifts of the one who loves us. Salvation, therefore, does not appear merely as a process of liberation, but is also an active acceptance of a duty. It is not only the expectation of a new state of life, but a decision to accept it and put it into practice. The witness of faith demands just this free decision and the witness that fails to arouse it is void of efficacy.

At the centre of society, then, there is a nucleus of believers who must serve as a constant stimulus to renewal. There is a perpetual crisis for those who sink into compliance with the present situation, treating it as final, having no confidence in the possibility of bringing about the liberation of mankind from enslavement to the past, from evil and death.

Witness requires a continual conversion in regard to social relations, based on a greater love of our fellow men, a sense of justice more demanding than our own, a life richer than our own existence. The witness of faith in Christ's resurrection, that is, in the liberating power of the Spirit, can be realized only by a community living in freedom.

Only when a new people is born, and establishes a new relationship between men, is it possible to believe in a love that will free mankind and lead it into a kingdom still to come.

On the other hand, the witness of a certain period of time or of a particular group of people is not enough to demonstrate the definitive freedom of the human community as a whole; it is unable to give us a glimpse of that destiny to which we are called.

The Church is wholly conscious of the need to be fully Catholic, that is, to reflect all the experiences of mankind, preserve the rich treasures of all cultures, and to express itself in all languages; otherwise the witness will be unable to foretell the future of its freedom.

II. Witness constantly renewed

The witness of faith will not, in the course of time, remain the same in its content, even though it recalls the same events, and is always concerned with the salvation of men. The gift of God was finally made known in Christ, but it will manifest itself with greater emphasis and wealth of meaning according to the manner in which it is accepted in our time. Every stage in our liberation leads to a fresh one, and all genuine practical experience of freedom enlarges the horizon of man's existence. Every day should bring a new message, and with it fresh witnesses to give it vividness and credibility.

The Christian witness, however, should not enclose itself up in formulas; it should not be the exclusive possession of one separate group. If its message is valid for all men and for all times, it can, when appropriately presented and experienced, become a possession shared in common with others. Once the Christian has arrived at this point he loses his exclusiveness in regard to the message of freedom; he derives it straight from Christ. But it is just this that makes it for a Christian a constant and ever renewed inspiration of liberty. If Christ is the absolute word of God in all the conditions of our present life, witness must enable man to discover new stages to which he must progress; it will encourage a critical attitude in the individual part and in mankind as a whole.

For mankind this is the witness of faith. It cannot fully justify all its promises; the values attached to it must be accepted even if their significance and scope cannot be completely verified. There is, so to speak, a kind of wager with existence and history. The point of reference lies in one's religious experience of Christ. There can be no turning back, no rejection of the present as a failure; one must have confidence in a love which has not yet revealed itself in all its fullness. It is impossible for us to turn to the future as offering complete freedom, unless we put our trust in a love which has not yet been made completely evident.

Accordingly, the witness of faith does not offer proofs of facts which have been asserted; it does not pretend to know their secrets; nor, on the other hand, does it reveal fundamentals or grant a foretaste of the blessings to be expected from a life of freedom.

Only a community based on the love of God revealed in Christ can live in freedom and, perceiving the riches of the future, is capable of preaching man's salvation.

For freedom to be possible it is not enough to say that it is necessary. For man to be completely saved it is not enough to preach the fact; it must be translated into action.

Apostolic witnesses are not only those who take up the challenge offered to them by Christ, who face the problems of existence without seeing completely how they must strive to turn them into actuality. Precisely because of this, the declaration of liberty demands a witness of faith, not only looking back to the past (the process of liberation), but above all waiting in trust for what has not yet come about. The future cannot be described because it has not yet been experienced, and can therefore only be prefigured in the fullness of the present. Faith is intertwined with all the temporal affairs of man as he lives in society.

III. The Apostolic Nature of Faith

The apostolic preaching required witnesses precisely because its content was not completely formulated; it found its full expression gradually as existence disclosed all its vicissitudes.

To be apostolic does not mean thinking exactly as did the apostles and the first Christians. It means proclaiming the same liberation of mankind, recalling the coming of Christ and the experience of his active presence. Faith is apostolic when it proclaims the liberty to which we are called through Christ's active, living presence. Apostolic quality is often thought of as an intellectual testimony, as an uninterrupted transmission from the earliest times to the present day, but this view is inadequate. The apostolic nature of the Church's message is not derived entirely from the past. Its intellectual content, indeed, is changed in the course of centuries, and is in fact bound to change. What the formulas express is far greater than what we can comprehend, experience, or describe in words.

There is a continuous relation with the past because it refers to the same mystery of which the apostles were the first witnesses. But our witness is not just a continuation of the apostles' witness except in so far as it discovers new means of preaching man's future in virtue of the life that Christ lived. Our bond with them is not created by time or intellectual contents, but by two essential conditions: the salvation of man (the nature of which remains uncertain), and the remembrance of the love of God made known to us in Christ. When these two conditions are present then we have apostolic witness. And since this fact can only be established by the community of the faithful, it follows that the basis of the apostolic witness must be an actual relationship with the Church. Hence, although the fact of witness is not indeed derived from the apostles through links in an unbroken chain, it is no less apostolic if it looks to the future of man as founded on the love of God as manifested in Christ, which compels our belief in the liberating love of all those who call upon him.

IV. THE BISHOP AS WITNESS OF THE FAITH

If we take these brief remarks about faith as our starting-point, as the witness of freedom proclaimed by Christ, it is easy to give an outline, even if it is general and therefore in somewhat vague terms, of the bishop considered as a witness to the faith.

1. *Witness of the Community*

If the Gospel is effectively proclaimed by a community living in freedom, the bishop is a witness to the faith in so far as he himself is an echo of that living experience of those believers who in a particular place receive the gift of the Spirit. A witness can only exist if he is in relation to a community living out its faith and giving it effective expression in the conditions of its own culture. If faith comes to life in a community the bishop can only be a witness to it if he reflects it faithfully.

Accordingly, the bishop became the true and authentic spokesman of the experience of salvation in his own community; hence he states those formulas of the faith which the word of God inspires in the actual conditions in which he lives.

In his relations with the universal Church he is the guarantor of the authenticity of the faith as expressed in his own community, and of the forms in which it is expressed.

Viewing this function against its historical background, we can take as an example the bishops assembled at the Council of Chalcedon, who were so many witnesses of the experiences of the faithful in their own communities, facing the whole Church, past and future, and being the announcers of those forms in which the word of God had been expressed, as lived and transmitted in that age.

In the same way the bishops of The Netherlands, in due proportion, should be considered as the witnesses to the faith as experienced in their own communities, lived and transmitted "in Dutch".

The apostolic character of the bishops' witness is stated and given verbal expression in reference to their own community, whose experiences they communicate to other communities. But in order that this function, in accord with the other communities, should effectively attain to a universal witness, certain conditions must be fulfilled. First of all, the experience of faith in the community must be genuine, that is, it must be the living experience, lived through in all its significance for man's salvation. This genuineness (and its scope) is warranted by the witness given by the other communities.

We cannot require each bishop to proclaim his witness in its universal validity; *primarily he is the witness for his own community*, within the bounds of the universal Church. Thus he has to proclaim the verbal formulas in which God's word has been embodied in the living conditions of his own environment and his own culture. To the degree, however, in which the experience of his own community is partial, incomplete or impaired by sin, the bishop's witness must be brought into harmony with all the others so as to arrive at a catholic witness, which alone is the effective and authentic expression of God's word in our present age.

This function accordingly requires from the bishop the capacity to confront all the other witnesses all over the world, including those who come from the past, so as to be prepared for the conversion of his own church, and to be open to the influence of such developments as the future may demand.

As the witness for his own community confronted with all the others, the bishop therefore becomes the means of universalizing the experience of faith pertaining to his own people.

It is here that the verbal forms given to God's word in a particular community undergo the searching process of the other communities, whose influence is so exerted that the formulation definitely acquires the character of authenticity.

The guarantee of the witness of faith of the individual bishops remains provisional and incomplete; in fact, it depends on the life of faith in his own community, receiving its confirmation only in contact with the experiences of all the other Christian communities.

But for this to be realized in practice, a second condition must be complied with: that the bishop faithfully reflects the experience of faith in his own community.

The bishop's chief duty in his contacts with the other Christian communities is that he shall be "faithful", that he shall pass on the verbal forms in his own community in all their completeness.

Therefore the bishop must above all be *a hearer*. He must know how to detect all the modulations which the word of God takes on in his own community, in the varying conditions of life and according to its different demands.

The bishop is not in possession of the secret of truth or life, in that he cannot *a priori* determine the whole significance of God's word. This he can do only to the extent that he makes himself aware of all the diverse formulations which God's word takes on within his own community. The truth to which the Spirit leads the whole Church (Jn. 14. 25; 16. 13) and to which the Spirit gives fundamental witness (Jn. 14. 25; Acts 1. 8), is not made plain by a manipulation of intellectual formulations, but only by the acceptance of the existence of the liberating power of the Spirit under all sorts of conditions. If intimacy with the Spirit is lacking, the witness becomes meaningless and the word of God is made vain, whatever the quarter from which it comes.

Hence the place where the truth is brought to light is not the theologian's desk or the orator's pulpit—even if he is a bishop—but the life lived by those who welcome the gift of God and make known all the depths of its potentiality.

The apostolic charisma, however, does not exempt the bishop from the duty of study, or from constant listening to the word of God (see *Dei Verbum*, 10). It lays this duty on him. The place at which the analysis is made is not the written word or codified formularies, but the whole diversity of existence. The bishop's words will be the fruit of human wisdom, but they will set limits to the power of God (see 1 Cor. 2. 4–5) if they do not re-echo the witness of the Spirit (Acts 5. 32) as it emerges from the life of faith. The bishop can call to witness the formulations made in former centuries and in other places, or mainly from his own individual faith (if it is capable of existing outside a living communion with the faithful). But this is not testimony to the word of God which is the people's salvation. In this sense, the bishop also belongs to the Church which listens and learns, to the Church which loves in the expectation of the definite return of God's Word.

The conviction that the episcopal charisma provides the bishop with a new source of knowledge or a secret means of making judgments is contradicted by the most elementary principles of ecclesiology. But it is a constant temptation to Gnosticism within Christian society. The criterion for witness is always the same for everyone; the word of God as it is manifested in the life of the Church and the constant working of the Spirit leading mankind to the land of freedom. Because of this, the bishop, as witness to the faith of the apostles, is fundamentally a man who waits and listens.

To determine the method and technical means of his listening, we must get to know the ways in which the Spirit acts. They cannot be known beforehand or put into some absolute category. But we know that they are many and varied. (See Jn. 3. 8–13; *Lumen gentium* 7. 12; *Ad gentes* 4. 23.) Therefore, as a witness, the bishop must be aware of all manifestations of the Spirit within his own community; he has the obligation not to "quench the Spirit who distributes his gifts as he pleases" (*Lumen gentium* 25. 12). The bishop as witness must be the sensitive part of his own community; the centre where the various charismata come together, are perceived and listened to faithfully, to the benefit of the universal Church. It is the bishop who gives a meaning to the life of his community, and so supplies a correct interpretation as to make it comprehensible to the whole Church. There must be a continuous contact among the various charismata, and a profound life of faith, so as not to give way to solutions of ready-made facts, of experiences already tested elsewhere; there must be no *a priori* rejection of any new point of view. With this as his mission the bishop is obliged to "take the part of his own community". This requires an especial loyalty to his own "territory" when he goes forth from it to face outsiders; this loyalty is not entirely free from risks. This is the origin of the dramatic kind of life the bishop must live; he must be faithful to his own community, but at the same time inspire in it a real and vital communion with all the other communities. In this way, he becomes, within his own community, the spokesman for all the other communities.

2. *Witness for the Community*

Each and every community of the faithful requires a contact and confrontation with the other communities. None is sufficient to itself. The bishop in communion with the other bishops is a

link in a chain of profound communion of faith which is included in all the different institutions of the life of the Church.
He *is* the one centre in which all the other ecclesiastical communities come face to face; he is therefore in a decisive situation
in regard to his own community. He does not, however, occupy
this decisive position automatically through his episcopal consecration, but through his relation with God's word as experienced
and formulated by the other communities.

This bond is not limited to the present time, but embraces all
the past, for each community lives by its own history. In this way,
within his own community, the bishop becomes a witness to the
power of salvation as revealed in history and actually manifested
in other conditions of life. He is the essentially catholic man,
and therefore attached to tradition. Often this task laid upon him
is understood as one of conserving the deposit of formulated doctrines, of exact intellectual statements. If the faith is considered
exclusively as adherence to the truth, its conservation can be reduced to a simple recording of doctrines and ideas. But if the
faith is interpreted as the acceptance of the transforming power
of the Spirit, which is operative in different dimensions and in
a multiplicity of forms, the task of witnessing to the faith becomes
rather a striving to prevent the richness of the past from being
diminished by the inertia of the present, making of individual
experiences an absolute standard. In fact, one can easily be
tempted to raise one's own experiences into an absolute rule of
faith; just as it is easy for a local community to believe that they
are faithfully interpreting the requirements of the whole Church.

The bishop becomes the centre of communion, and the judge
of the genuineness of the experience of faith. This is not because
he possesses the secret and guarantee of such experience, but because, by virtue of his episcopal function, he is the centre at
which all the experiences of the local community are gathered.

He is unfaithful to this duty if, believing himself alone to be
in possession of the right of absolute judgment about the faith,
he does not listen to the other Christian communities, but shuts
himself up in his present geographical situation. Before his own
people he must appear as a faithful witness to the others.

When the Church was composed of small communities it was
easy to arrive at a catholic position, even if it did not reflect a

variety of different cultures and different languages. Today it has become much harder because the Church has become universal. This is the reason why the bishop, as focal point of the catholic faith of the Church, is required to have a profound and sensitive awareness of the universal, so as to catch the echoes of the life of faith under present-day conditions. Similarly, when the apostles' witness carried the burden of few experiences, there were few things to be remembered, and not many to discover. The road to the future indeed involves a profound recovery of the past. Only a man with a long memory will be successful in taking a long view, which he gains in virtue of all that he remembers.

When the past was of small dimensions, remembrance consisted in "conserving", but now it is long, remembrance can only be recovered by recourse to the future; it brings to light many new experiences which draw upon riches of what has occurred but has not yet been explored.

As the witness of faith in his own community, the bishop today can be nothing less than the inspirer of renewal; he cannot conserve without making fresh discoveries. There is so much to remember that the bishop cannot pass it on without stimulating new and vital experiences.

In former times it was possible to preserve the faith by enclosing it in fixed forms; today we have the contrary situation. In order to pass on the message of salvation it is necessary to change its content according to new historical situations. So the bishop must be the guide in this constant renewal of the existential forms of the faith.

As a witness to salvation accepted in hope, the bishop must become the agent of renewal for his people, so that the freedom he has proclaimed always corresponds to the changing conditions of life.

If faith today is difficult, it is because it is developing in an age of prophetic witness. The witnesses of past events are no longer sufficient (even if there has ever been a time when they sufficed); now there is far greater need of witnesses for God who is to come. The bishop, as a witness to faith, must not be only a sign of what has been, but the pointer to what is to come, lest other witnesses arise and sacramental institutions find themselves in conflict with hierarchical institutions—which often happens when the age is one of rapid change.

To avert this, it is necessary for Christian communities to evolve a new conception of the bishop, and above all not to put obstacles in the way of many bishops' proposals for renewal—which should not stop at the feet of their thrones, but embrace the whole life of faith.

The new type of bishop cannot be invented by theologians or bureaucrats, but must issue from new communities of the faith, if they live with a consciousness of their mission in the world. The one thing essential is to encourage, or at least not hinder, this new birth—as gentle as are all the works of the Spirit.

Translated by Alec Randall

Georg Wagner

The Bishop in Eastern Orthodox Theology

IF WE look in the writings of the Apostle Paul for an answer to the question, "What is the Church?", we get one main answer: "The Church is the body of Christ" (1 Cor. 12. 27, etc.). Again, if we ask, "What is the Eucharist?", we get the answer, "... the body of Christ" (cf. 1 Cor. 11. 24). The Church is the body of Christ and the Eucharist is the body of Christ. Of course "body" in each statement has a slightly different meaning; the "ecclesial" body of Christ and the "sacramental" body of Christ cannot simply be identified. And yet the one reality without the other is inconceivable.

It is its communion in the body and blood of the Lord which makes the Church the body of Christ. The Eucharist is the central mystery of the Church. Of course, only those can participate in the mystery who have entered by the door of baptism, and participation in the sacraments itself demands constant attention to the call of God which reaches us through the preaching of the word. The sacramental community with Christ must be constantly strengthened by the Christian's imitation of Christ in his daily life: "If you keep my commandments, you will abide in my love" (Jn. 15. 10). But the Eucharist is the centre of Christian life: "He who eats my flesh and drinks my blood abides in me and I in him" (Jn. 6. 56). The Eucharist is the central event not only in the life of the individual Christian, but the existence of the Church as such, as the body of Christ: "Because there is one bread, we who are many are one body, for we all partake of the one bread" (1 Cor. 10. 17). This one bread is the body of Christ.

I. Eucharistic Ecclesiology

Such an understanding of the New Testament statements about the Church and the Eucharist leads to a characteristic view of the mystery of the Church. The Orthodox canonist and Church historian, Archpriest Nicholas Afanassieff, who died in Paris in 1966, calls this view of the Church, significantly, a "eucharistic ecclesiology".[1] It is by no means a closed system worked out to the last detail, but a determined attempt to understand the authentic Eastern Orthodox tradition in the field of ecclesiology. This tradition is preserved in liturgies, in the statements of the Fathers, and not least in the decrees of Orthodox councils. The "eucharistic ecclesiology" which is found in these sources provides a fruitful contrast to the ecclesiological positions of the dogmatics manuals of the last three centuries—positions which were largely taken over from Western Scholasticism. This fact alone indicates that Afanassieff's work puts us in contact with the authentic Orthodox tradition.

1. *The Starting-point: the Eucharistic Assembly*

To remain true to its principles, a "eucharistic ecclesiology" must start from particular individual communities which assemble in a particular place to celebrate the Eucharist. Until the return of the Lord, the eucharistic assembly is always an event in this or that place. From the earliest times, Christians have seen the Eucharist as the fulfilment of the prophecy of Malachi (1. 11) that "a pure offering" would be made "in every place" instead of the old offering in the Temple at Jerusalem, in which God no longer took pleasure.[2] The New Testament knows no concentration of worship at one place on the earth comparable to that in the Old Testament at the Temple of Jerusalem. God the Father does not now wish to be worshipped either on Mount Gerizim or in the Temple at Jerusalem (Jn. 4. 21). The Temple of Jerusalem has been replaced by the body of Christ, the Church, which assembles in every place in the power of the Holy Spirit (cf. Jn. 2. 19–21). This temple is present above all where the Eucharist

---

[1] Afanassieff's major work has only just been published (in Russian), N. Afanassieff, *Cerkov' Ducha Svjatago* (The Church of the Holy Spirit) (Paris, 1971).

[2] Justin, *Dialogue with Trypho*, chap. 41; *Didache*, chap. 14.

is celebrated. The Church's continued existence in scattered units, in the "diaspora", is even a necessary condition of its mission in the time between the ascension and the return of the Lord.

This situation of the Church on earth is reflected in the texts of the old liturgies. In the Byzantine liturgy of Chrysostom the "First Prayer of the Faithful" speaks of the ministers of the altar calling on God "in all times and all places", and the great eucharistic prayer begins with the joyful assertion: "It is right and fitting to praise you, . . . to give thanks to you, to call upon you in every place where you rule." The same ideas lie behind the familiar phrases of Roman Prefaces, *tibi semper et ubique gratias agere*, "that we should always and everywhere give thanks to you".

In each local church Christ is present with the fullness of his truth and grace, just as each particle of the broken eucharistic bread in the body of Christ entire. But we should not think of the individual local churches as self-sufficient and separate units. The *koinonia* or *communio* of the individual local churches with each other is the result of their inner unity, based on that which constitutes the life of each of them. The body of Christ is always and everywhere the same, wherever it may be present. And the apostolic faith is similarly the same whenever and wherever it is preached without distortion. When this inner unity exists, there is also a need for an external community of the local churches with each other, because they are—all together and each in itself —the one Church. Nevertheless, we should not forget in all this that the Church on earth is always found primarily in the form of the particular *ekklesia*, assembling in this or that place to be made the body of Christ by the Eucharist.

2. *The Bishop as the President of the Eucharist Assembly*

The oldest detailed description we have of a Christian Eucharist comes from Justin Martyr around the middle of the second century.[3] This description mentions the "president of the brethren" who, after the readings from Scripture, addresses the assembly and later pronounces the eucharistic prayer over the bread and cup. Justin in his account makes a clear distinction

[3] Justin, *Apologia* I, chaps. 65 and 67, H. Bettenson, *Documents of the Christian Church* (London, New York, Toronto, 1963), pp. 93-5.

between the "general" or common prayers, in which the whole community takes a direct and active part, and the eucharistic prayer over the bread and cup, which is said by the president alone. According to Justin's description, the community's participation in this prayer is expressed only by the "Amen" said by all at the end. We do not know how the community in Justin's time usually described the office of their "president", but if we go back several decades to the letters of Ignatius, the martyr bishop of Antioch, we find that Justin's "president" performs the same functions that Ignatius describes to the *episkopos*. Ignatius makes a number of references to the "bishop", in passages which discuss the Eucharist.[4] It is the bishop who normally presides at the celebration of the Eucharist and says the eucharistic prayer: "Let that be considered a valid eucharist which is celebrated by the bishop, or by one whom he appoints."[5] Of course the bishops of Ignatius' time had little in common with the prelates of the high Middle Ages or the Baroque; in many respects a more appropriate comparison would be with the priest in charge of a very large parish.

II. "Monarchical" Episcopate or Collegial Leadership of a Local Community?

Ignatius is the first clear witness to the exercise of episcopal authority by an individual over a local community. In contrast, Paul refers at the beginning of his Epistle to the Philippians (1. 1) to "bishops" (plural, *episkopoi*) and "deacons" in a local community. The clear impression given by our oldest sources is that individual local communities were governed, not by one man, but by a college. This impression is confirmed when we realize that in the earliest period the expressions *episkopos* and *presbyteros* are clearly synonymous.[6] The use of the word *episkopos* as a technical term to describe a single "president", who was the head of the local community and led the eucharistic assembly, can thus be traced back only as far as Ignatius, or the beginning of the second century. Does this mean that the same is true of the office which the word describes, or did the thing itself—

[4] Ignatius, Eph. 5. 2; 20. 2; Philad. 4; Smyrn. 12. 2.
[5] Ignatius, Smyrn. 8. 1 (Loeb. ed.); Bettenson, *Documents*, p. 90.
[6] Cf. Acts 20. 17, 28; Tit. 1. 5, 7.

without the description which later became traditional—in fact
exist before?

1. *The Leadership of the Primitive Community in Jerusalem*

Turning to the account (Acts 1–12) of the primitive community in Jerusalem, we find a relatively clear picture of a
special pastoral ministry exercised by one man, Peter. His special
ministry within the Jerusalem community corresponds to the
commission which he received from the Lord (cf. Lk. 22. 32;
Jn. 21. 15–17). It is even legitimate to see Peter's pastoral ministry in Jerusalem as the model for the ministry of all later
bishops. They perform in their communities the ministry which
Peter exercised in Jerusalem. Peter's pastoral ministry in Jerusalem was later taken over by James, and James is regarded by
tradition as the first bishop of Jerusalem.

But Peter in Jerusalem was a member of a college, that of the
eleven other apostles. The account of Pentecost in Acts describes
Peter as "standing with the eleven" (2. 14). This college is clearly
so important that the restoration of the full complement of its
members—through the election of Matthias—is the first event re-
ported in Acts after the ascension (Acts 1. 15 ff.). We may well
ask whether in Luke's plan of the Acts of the Apostles the restoration of the complement of the apostolic college is not an
essential precondition for the descent of the Spirit on the Church
at Pentecost.

In time "elders" (*presbyteroi*) join the apostles (Acts 11. 30;
15. 2–23; 16. 4); and, just as at the beginning of Acts Peter
appears with the college of the eleven other apostles, so towards
the end (Acts 21. 18) we find James surrounded by a college of
presbyters.

Such a council of elders had a firm precedent in the tradition
of Old Testament Judaism. Its most important biblical model is
probably the account in Numbers of the seventy elders who
assisted Moses: "Gather for me seventy men of the elders of
Israel", says God to Moses, "... and I will take some of the
spirit which is upon you and put it upon them; and they shall
bear the burden of the people with you, that you may not bear it
yourself alone" (Num. 11. 16–17; cf. 11. 25–30).

2. *Evidence from the History of the Liturgy*

Significantly, the oldest prayer which has come down to us from the ordination of a presbyter (from Hippolytus, at the beginning of the third century) makes a clear reference to this story in Numbers: "Look upon this your servant and grant him the spirit of grace and counsel for the presbytery, ... as you commanded Moses to choose elders so that you might fill them with the spirit which you bestowed on your servant Moses."[7] Just as the seventy elders shared the gift of prophecy and the burden which Moses carried, so the council of presbyters shares in the charism and responsibility entrusted to the bishop. Hence the special pastoral office of one man and the college of concelebrants, assistants and representatives of that one man are not mutually exclusive, but complementary.

We can trace the special office of one man at the centre of a college of fellow pastors as far back as the beginnings of the church at Jerusalem. In contrast, we have no similarly clear references to the existence of a "monarchical episcopate" in the earliest times. We may, however, ask whether the special pastoral office of an individual was not, here too, a necessity, and one which must have originated from the form of the eucharistic assembly.

The episcopal office is in the first place a liturgical ministry. In the eyes of the whole of Christian antiquity—for Cyprian and for John Chrysostom—the bishop is the priest (*sacerdos, hiereus*) of the Church in the immediate sense. Before separate parishes came into existence, the bishop normally presided at the celebration of the Eucharist, and when the bishop's church finally split into separate parishes with presbyters at the head, it remained the ideal that he should be the actual celebrant of the Eucharist. It is the task of the president of the eucharistic celebration to say the eucharistic prayer over the bread and cup, as Christ said the thanksgiving over the bread and cup at the Last Supper. In antiquity, however, the eucharistic prayer could only be said by one person. A form of concelebration in which all the presbyters recited the eucharistic prayer together would have been impossible at that time for purely technical reasons. Until the last part of the fourth century, the Church possessed no fixed written

[7] Hippolytus, *Traditio apostolica*, chap. 7.

liturgical texts. Basil the Great (about 375) apparently includes the entire eucharistic prayer among the contents of oral tradition,[8] clearly because—before his time—there were no fixed written texts of this prayer. Hippolytus, at the beginning of the third century, clearly states that the texts of liturgical prayers which he gives are to be regarded simply as models, not as binding formularies.[9] And, in the middle of the second century, Justin says that the "president of the brethren" says the eucharistic prayer "to the best of his ability".[10] It seems therefore that the eucharistic prayer and the other liturgical prayers must have been said extempore and, to a certain extent—within the limits of a constant tradition—rephrased on each occasion. Naturally this could only happen if there were a single speaker. Normally this function would be performed by the bishop.

In fact, in Hippolytus' description, the bishop alone says the eucharistic prayer, while all the presbyters stretch out their hands over the bread and cup with him.[11] This image of the concelebration of the presbyterium with its bishop, eloquently expressed in a silent gesture, corresponds to the participation of the presbyterium in what the bishop does, as described in the prayer at a presbyter's ordination already quoted from Hippolytus.

3. *"The Bishop's Council"*[12]

The same relationship is reflected in the seating arrangements for formal assemblies of the church. The bishop alone occupies the cathedra in the centre of the apse. No one else may take this seat; if the bishop is absent it remains empty. The seats in the apse on each side of the bishop—or of the empty cathedra—are reserved for the presbyterium. The bishop alone presides, in conjunction with his presbyters: "the bishop presiding in the place of God and the presbyters in the place of the council of the apostles", as Ignatius of Antioch describes it.[13] The presbyters, alongside the bishop, are "those who preside over you".[14]

[8] Basil, *de Spiritu Sancto*, chap. 27 (*PG* 32, 188D).
[9] Hippolytus, *Traditio apostolica*, chap. 9.
[10] Justin, *Apologia* I, chap. 67 (Bettenson, *Documents*, p. 95); cf. *Didache*, chap. 10 (Bettenson, p. 91).
[11] Hippolytus, *Traditio apostolica*, chap. 4.
[12] Cf. Ignatius, Philad. 8. 1.
[13] Ignatius, Magn. 6. 1.
[14] Ignatius, Magn. 6. 2.

We have become accustomed to regard Ignatius as primarily the champion of the "monarchical episcopate", and therefore easily forget the important position he gives to the presbyterium. Ignatius, in fact, calls for submission not merely to the bishop but to the presbyterium.[15] The bishop presides in the place of Christ or of God the Father, and the "crown" of presbyters which surrounds him[16] corresponds to the apostolic college. Ignatius compares the presbyterium with the college of apostles, but applies the comparison in the opposite direction, and calls the apostles the "presbytery of the Church".[18]

"Let all respect... the presbyters as the council (*synedrion*) of God and the college (*syndesmos*) of apostles."[19] In this connection, it is interesting to find that the Jewish Supreme Council, the Sanhedrin in Jerusalem, is sometimes called *presbyterion* or "council of elders" (Lk. 22. 66; Acts 22. 5). The word *synedrion* throws new light on the meaning of "presbyterium": the presbyters are like the assistants or assessors who sit with the presiding judge when a court is in session. Such "assessors" are even included in the biblical conception of the eschatological tribunal of God and the Messiah.[20] Christ says to the apostles, "When the Son of man shall sit on his glorious throne, you who have followed me will also sit on twelve thrones, judging the twelve tribes of Israel" (Mt. 19. 28). In Luke's account of the Last Supper we find the theme of participation in judgment combined with the other theme of fellowship at the table: "... that you may eat and drink at my table in my kingdom, and sit on thrones judging the twelve tribes of Israel" (Lk. 22. 30). And in Revelation (4. 4, etc.) we see around the thrones of God and the Lamb the thrones of the twenty-four elders, in whom we are probably meant to see the "elders" of the New and Old Covenants, the patriarchs and the apostles.

At the divine judgment, the role of the "assessors" is naturally limited to that of official witnesses to the exercise of divine justice. The position of the "assessors" in the assembly of the earthly

[15] Ignatius, Eph. 2. 2; 20. 2; Magn. 2; 7. 1; Trall. 2. 2; 13. 2.
[16] Ignatius, Magn. 13. 1.
[17] Ignatius, Magn. 6. 1; Trall. 2–3.
[18] Ignatius, Philad. 5. 1.
[19] Cf. Ignatius, Trall. 3. 1.
[20] Cf. Is. 24. 23; Dan. 7. 9; Rev. 20. 4.

ekklesia is quite different. Since the president here is a fallible and mortal man, his ministry stands in continual need of the collegial support of the members of the presbyterium. If the bishop is sick or absent, the presbyters act for him; when he dies they maintain the continuity of the pastoral office until there is a new occupant for the bishop's chair. But, above all, the presbyterium should be a real council around the bishop; its members should support and supplement the bishop's ministry with advice and action. To a large extent, we have to rediscover this role and implement it in the ordinary life of the Church.

According to Ignatius, without bishop, presbyterium and deacons there is no Church.[21] Presbyterium and diaconate are ministries equally important—or almost—in the life of the Church as the episcopate. We have previously compared the bishop in the early Church with a modern parish priest. In fact, the bishop of the early Church and the parish priest of today are both leaders of particular local communities, and especially presidents of their eucharistic assemblies. And yet there is an important difference. The bishop is surrounded by his presbyterium, but in the parish there is no presbyterium in the sense of a genuine college of fellow pastors. For this reason the parish has to look for its completion to the diocesan church. This is probably the most important reason for the canonical dependence of the parish on the diocesan church, and for the growth of the diocese as a group of churches comprising a number of separate communities.

In any case, after initial variations, it has become an established practice of the Church to appoint, not a bishop, but simply a priest as president in places where "a single presbyter alone suffices".[22] Perhaps we should see this too as evidence that the "monarchical" episcopate always needs to be supplemented by a college of presbyters. When there is no presbyterium there is no bishop to preside in the local *ekklesia* within the circle of his presbyters.

[21] Ignatius, Trall. 3. 1; cf. 7. 2.
[22] Cf. Canon 6 of the Council of Sardica (343/344).

Translated by Francis McDonagh

Norbert Brox

The Conflict between Anicetus and Polycarp

THE names of Bishops Anicetus of Rome and Polycarp of Smyrna are associated with one of the first phases of the dispute about Easter in the early Church, which still constituted a stubborn problem for church unity at Nicaea (325), and even later. More exactly, both bishops belong to the prehistory[1] of the real controversy, since the (in our present condition) relevant aspect of the negotiations they conducted in Rome shortly after 150 is precisely the fact that actual conflict was avoided.

I. UNITY IN QUESTION

The problem centred upon the fact that churches in Asia Minor and neighbouring territories—like the Jews—celebrated the feast of Easter, whatever the day of the week, on the fourteenth day of Nisan (the "Quartodeciman" usage), and differed in this practice from the great majority of all other churches, which celebrated Easter on the following Sunday. This difference of church practice in the treatment of the central paschal mystery, having persisted without question for decades, suddenly became a real dilemma for the whole Church, probably because the Quartodeciman Christians intermixed with others and the contrast had a disturbing effect within a narrow compass.[2] The

[1] A. Hilgenfeld, *Der Paschastreit der alten Kirche* (Halle, 1860), pp. 227–250, calls it a "prelude".
[2] In the scholarly dispute on this question, I share the view that in general it was always a matter between Rome and Asia Minor of the date

question arose whether church unity could tolerate or must exclude these ritual variations. In the discussions at Rome between Anicetus and Polycarp, as the representatives of the divergent calendars, this was the most important and the most difficult problem. Whereas it proved possible to resolve other difficulties, this one remained without agreement, since neither of the two parties felt itself to be in a position, nor saw any reason, to surrender its own usage and adopt that of the other for the sake of unity. Nevertheless, this did not involve them in conflict proper; there was nothing approaching a schism. The unity of the Church persisted despite ritual variations in the observance of fasting and the celebration of Easter. As a sign of peace, Anicetus allowed the Asiatic bishop to celebrate the Eucharist at his side in the Roman church.

The events are known from Eusebius (beginning of the fourth century) (*HE*, IV, 14. 1; V, 24. 14–17), and in this respect he draws mainly (or even exclusively) on Irenaeus (end of the second century). Therefore we possess no direct testimonies, and the different later reports tend to vary in emphasis according to their own situations.[3] But the facts are reliably established as already described. In this matter, church unity became a problem around the middle of the second century inasmuch as there were differing usages in regard to important church practices, but not because of divergent doctrine (even though there were some differences here, too). In any case, there was probably a quite distinct theology of Easter at the basis of the deviant Easter observance: the Quartodeciman supporters probably thought of themselves as celebrating mainly the memorial of the death of Christ, whereas the celebration on the following Sunday certainly stood expressly

---

and not of the treatment of Easter, which was, apparently, not yet celebrated in Rome at that time—a view that, following upon H. Koch, K. Müller, K. Holl, H. Lietzmann, *et al.*, e.g., M. Richard, "La question pascale au IIe siècle", *L'Orient Syrien* 6 (1961), pp. 179–212; *Zeitschrift f.d.neutest.Wiss.* 56 (1965), pp. 270–2; and W. Huber, *Passa und Ostern* (Berlin, 1969), pp. 55–60, again put forward. For a different view, see, e.g., B. Lohse, *Das Passafest der Quartadecimaner* (Gütersloh, 1953), pp. 114 ff.; Chr. Mohrmann, "Le conflit pascal au IIe siècle. Note philologique", *VigChrist* 16 (1962), pp. 154–71; P. Nautin, *Lettres et écrivains chrétiens des IIe et IIIe siècles* (Paris, 1967), pp. 80–4.

[3] Cf. N. Brox, "Altkirchliche Formen des Anspruchs auf apostolische Kirchenverfassung, *Kairos* NF 12 (1970) (pp. 113–40), pp. 122–8.

for the resurrection.[4] In addition, the question of the date of celebration was very soon connected with the necessary demarcation
of the Church from Judaism, so that the Quartodeciman faction
could have counted as dangerously Judaizing Christians. Therefore there were probably objective differences at work too. Nevertheless, it is impossible (and this caused the difficulties in the following era) to view these differences as arising from a decadent
and subsequently deviant development on one of the two sides.
Both bishops were initially acquainted with their own usage
alone, on the basis of their individual traditions pure and simple.
It was communication between the local churches that made
them aware of the multiplicity of differences. Therefore the
problem of unity in the Church arose out of its own history and
the development of the component churches, and not primarily
from conflicting doctrine, division and heresy. In regard to the
situation of Polycarp and Anicetus, it must be remembered that
this circumstance became conscious knowledge in a phase of
church history in which, in doctrine and terminology, there
were as yet no pre-existing means for overcoming such difficulties. There was not the dogmatic theory of church unity and
continuity in the length and breadth of history which could, for
example, so explain the divergent Easter usage as to make it com-
patible with ecclesiastical unity. On the other hand, the difference in Easter practice was not seen as destroying or rendering
unity impossible, for Anicetus and Polycarp expressly demonstrated their ecclesiastical unity despite the fact that the question
remained open. They were still clearly without the dogmatic and
disciplinary formula which would enable such a conflict to be
resolved, and this in its turn helped to produce the kind of per-
plexity which allowed the case to hang fire. They were also without a corresponding legal structure which would have demanded
a submission of one church to the other *per se* (of the church of
Asia Minor to the church of Rome).[5] But this precisely would

---

[4] See C. Schmidt, *Gespräche Jesu mit seinen Jüngern nach der Aufer-
stehung* (Leipzig, 1919), pp. 577–725; J. Lebreton, *Histoire de l'Eglise* 2
(Paris, 1948), pp. 87 f.; W. Huber, *op. cit.*, pp. 1–88.

[5] This is so, even though the visit of Polycarp to Rome (instead of a
visit by Anicetus to Smyrna) may be evaluated as an indication of a pre-
existing recognition of the primacy of Rome: A. von Harnack, *Lehrbuch
der Dogmengeschichte I* (Tübingen, ⁴1909), p. 488.

seem to have been the basis of the possibility of an ecclesial (and not solely legally oriented) resolution of the conflict.

In any case, we learn nothing certain from the dogmatically interpreted criteria by which the confrontation between the two bishops was determined. We obtain reliable evidence only of the difference as a perceived problem, and of the fruitlessness of the attempt to solve it as a matter of principle (HE, V, 24. 16). What the report does offer is (as a comparison shows) the perspective of Irenaeus or, as the case may be, of Eusebius. According to this, the case was to be judged by the principle of apostolicity, which lays down that in the Church that which is of apostolic origin, and not merely that which is honourable and old, is in the right. The application of this principle to the Easter problem among the later theologians and church historians from Irenaeus by way of Eusebius up to Socrates (HE, V, 22) and Sozomen (HE, VII, 19) in the fifth century shows that it was conceived in too linear a fashion to be able to deal appropriately with the actual historical events, and that it was not always applicable without a certain partisanship.[6] It can certainly be said of both Anicetus and Polycarp that they had recourse to the reliable and unimpeachable tradition of their respective churches, though in the case of Anicetus it is uncertain whether he already appealed to the apostolic origin of the Sunday observance of Easter (which for Pope Victor at the end of the second century was not open to proof but as good as certain). According to Irenaeus, the Asia Minor Christians had apostolic tradition on their side, whereas Anicetus could appeal to the custom of his predecessors (HE, V, 24. 16); as the accompanying text indicates at several points, Eusebius was of the contrary opinion, that the Roman tradition possessed the apostolic quality, whereas all that the Asia Minor Christians possessed was a set of old traditions (HE, V, 23. 1; 24. 1, 11; 25). Anicetus and Polycarp obviously themselves left the question open in their confrontation of their local ecclesial traditions and usages, which allowed of no abrogation and lacked any formula which would have permitted theological classification. According to the testimony of the next generation (Irenaeus) this situation did not make impossible the unity and community

[6] Cf. N. Brox, loc. cit.

of the two churches, and did not raise them as issues on the dogmatic level.

II. UNITY AS THE PEACE OF THE WHOLE CHURCH

The practical solution which Polycarp and Anicetus agreed on was no resolution of the theoretical problem of an absence of ritual and theological unanimity, and was not a violent settlement of existing differences. The solution was seen as lying in the continuation and reinforcement of reciprocal recognition and tolerance, and thus in ecclesial peace. Eusebius cites the letter of Irenaeus to the later pope Victor, in which Irenaeus recalls for Victor the attitude of his predecessors Sixtus, Telesphorus, Hyginus, Pius and Anicetus: "Although they did not observe the same (i.e., the Quartodeciman usage) they enjoyed no less a degree of peace with those who came from communities in which the practice was retained. And yet the exercise of the usage must have had the effect of bringing a contrary observance to the attention of those who did not enjoy it" (HE, V, 24. 14).[7] When Irenaeus has portrayed in more detail the conflict between Anicetus and Polycarp and described the fruitlessness of their discussions, he continues: "Despite these differences, they remained in communion one with the other. And, out of respect, Anicetus allowed Polycarp to celebrate the Eucharist in his, Anicetus', church. And they took leave of one another in peace, in possession of the peace of the whole Church, whether they observed or did not observe the practice" (HE, V, 24. 17).[8]

Since we do not have access to the original documents, the precise conditions of this peace are unknown. Was it a question of a tolerant agreement until a further occasion, that is, until there was a chance of unification of church practice; or was this a fundamental affirmation of the multiform nature of the Church? That we do not know, yet we have reason to suspect that the first of the two alternatives fits the case. The only reliable tradition we have is that of a peace between the local churches assured under difficult conditions. Even if it were a question of a

[7] Translation from the German version according to Ph. Haeuser and H. A. Gärtner (Munich, 1967), p. 269.

[8] The last sentence in the well-founded translation by C. Andresen, *Zeitschrift f.d.neutest. Wiss.* 56 (1965), p. 257.

pragmatic peace, it would meet with unequivocal opposition: the peace of the whole Church was more important to the participants than the unification and uniformity of ritual procedure and the calendar. Hence there is here a more respectable version of ecclesial unity than is to be found in any centralizing co-ordination of local church images. For the sake of this unity, which favours peace, on each side there was a clear retraction of any absolute precedence in rank of the particular tradition (nevertheless held to be indispensable). In the case of the conflict between Anicetus and Polycarp, dogmatic unification would therefore seem to have been impossible and at the same time something not to be forced upon either party. They left the situation unclarified to that extent, and allowed church life to proceed as before in pluriformity and without any doctrinaire certainty. Precisely for this reason, they were praised some decades later by Irenaeus (and not by him alone) in the interest of the whole Church, and elevated as an ideal.

When, in the same matter, Pope Victor introduced into the controversy an attitude to the maintenance of Roman conceptions of unity and Roman claims that was different to that of his predecessors; when he demanded from the churches of Asia Minor their submission to the Roman church and therefore an abandonment of their own traditions; and when, finally, he even threatened excommunication: according to Eusebius' account by no means all bishops were able to accept this procedure as a measure conducive to unity. There were protests, and the "counter-claim" to Victor "to come down on the side of peace, unity and love" (HE, V, 24. 10), which they saw his method not as ensuring but, on the contrary, endangering. Among those who protested was the Gallican bishop Irenaeus, who, as far as usage was concerned, was, in fact, on Victor's side. From the fragments of his now often cited writings, we know that he would have preferred Victor to have continued the conduct of his predecessors (that is, that of Anicetus) in regard to the same matter. Eusebius reports: "He warns Victor with respect yet emphatically that he should not exclude entire churches of God, which hold to ancient, traditional usages", and continues: "... despite this difference, all these Christians lived in peace, and we too live in peace. *Variation in the observance of fastdays indicates unity in faith....*

People were never excluded for such reasons, but rather those who were presbyters before you, even though they did not follow the (Quartodeciman) usage, offered the Eucharist to those who had that usage and came from such communities" (HE, V, 24. 11, 13, 15). One ought to think and act like an Anicetus, and one may not break with a Polycarp, but must retain ecclesial communion with him. Because Irenaeus, even at the present time, holds this to be the only ecclesiastical and Christian procedure, he recalls and appeals to Anicetus' behaviour; it is only for that reason that we know of the incident. And Irenaeus sees no inconsistencies here, but applies the (admittedly somewhat paradoxical) ecclesial formula: "Variation in the observance of fast-days is a sign of unity of faith."[9] Anicetus and Polycarp are hereby confirmed in their action, and by a bishop and theologian who in his writings always shows practical sympathy for the basic formal principles of an ecclesiastical theology (as for instance apostolicity, tradition, teaching authority, unity of doctrine), and for the merits of the claims of Rome over the whole Church. Here again (and not as when he is dealing with heretics), Irenaeus unequivocally sets the peace of the whole Church above formal unanimities. In this, he manifests a certain liberality towards divergent developments within the Church. In any case, it should be remarked that Irenaeus is here advising reticence in Roman claims in regard to his own original church (Irenaeus came from Asia Minor), even though he was almost more firmly convinced of the rightness (that is, apostolicity) of every detail of those claims than of anything else.

The cardinal idea of diversity in unity, which Irenaeus drew from the behaviour of Anicetus and Polycarp, clearly continued to play a part whenever local churches tried to assert themselves against the Bishop of Rome. Firmilian of Caesarea in Cappadocia, in his quite caustic letter on the re-baptizing of heretics, written to St Cyprian in support of his campaign against Pope Stephen I, mentions that "also in most of the other provinces (i.e., not only in Rome) much is different in accordance with the variation of places and of men. Yet for that reason no one is ever torn from the peace and unity of the Catholic Church. This

[9] Eusebius, HE, V, 24. 13 (E. Schwartz, *Kleine Ausgabe* (Leipzig, [5]1955), p. 213.

Stephen has now dared to do by breaking the peace in your regard which his predecessors always preserved in reciprocal love and respect" (75. 6). In contradistinction to the express demand of Pope Stephen, Firmilian adheres to the "rule of truth and peace" (*regulam veritatis et pacis*) (75. 24),[10] which one might call a further short formula for the fundamental idea of the unity of the Church. By "rule" is meant a guiding line or canon of faith and church life, which is not only the truth as a single doctrine, but the mutual peace of the participant churches. Here the essential line has changed in comparison with that adopted by Irenaeus; it is polemical: Firmilian doubts not only the peaceful disposition of, but the possession of truth by, the Bishop of Rome. Otherwise, the idea of unity in diversity is connected, here too, with a reference to the Easter dispute. Perhaps it was closely involved with the Anicetus/Polycarp tradition.

Admittedly, in the course of history, this particular matter did not always feature thinking along the lines of the Anicetus/Polycarp outcome. Pope Victor already saw things in a different light. And in his later judgment on the Easter dispute, the church historian Socrates (fifth century) was on the side of the Emperor Constantine, who was interested in church uniformity for political reasons (cf. Eusebius, *Vita Constantini*, III, 18 f.), and, like Constantine, represented the pragmatic viewpoint that in cases such as the Easter dispute the minority should adopt the majority view, and multiformity must be sacrificed—which meant that minority usage was simultaneously made tantamount to heresy (Judaism).[11] A few years later, Sozomen, who had read Socrates' judgment, again adopts in his church history the more liberal view that a multiplicity of usages and traditions was always proper to the Church. He too states this in connection with the Easter dispute, and—despite his very imprecise historical knowledge—is aware that this dispute was settled by compromise at a very early stage: "Everyone was to celebrate the feast as he had been accustomed to do, without thereby being cut off from reciprocal communion"; and he adds: "For they justly held it

---

[10] Translation according to J. Niglutsch and A. Egger (Kempten, 1879), pp. 460 and 478; Text: CSEL III, 2 (G. Hartel: Vienna, 1871), pp. 813 and 825.

[11] Socrates, HE, V, 22 (PG 67, pp. 625-9).

to be foolish that for the sake of usage those should part who were agreed on the decisive concerns of religion. For one cannot find the same traditions—equal in every respect—in all churches, even when they enjoy the same faith."[12] Here, then, diversity and individuality of the component churches, together with basic unity of faith, are emphatically made part of the picture of the Church.

Anicetus and Polycarp, therefore (though in an obviously much less centralistically oriented Church), enjoyed and practised a conception of ecclesial unity which was consistently echoed by others. The "main thing in which they wanted no conflict was peace in the Church" is Irenaeus's comment (Eusebius, HE, V, 24. 16). For the sake of peace the strict uniformity of all component churches was to be surrendered. The diverse forms of ecclesial life and belief were allowed to persist even where they featured substantially relevant differences, when otherwise peace as the inalienable form of ecclesial unity would be endangered. Unity understood thus can exist, and be shown to exist, beyond differences, whereas it can be extinguished by enforcing uniformity in matters of detail. The three bishops Anicetus, Polycarp and—not much later—Irenaeus saw, in regard to the (then) serious matter of the conflict over the celebration of Easter, the task of the bishops and of the Bishop of Rome (to whom Irenaeus appeals) as lying not in the approximation of all churches to the one form (if necessary by excommunication) but in the practice of the "peace of the whole Church", and therefore of unity as communication and community, even under difficulties. Anicetus and Polycarp themselves accepted reciprocally what the later theologians I have cited stated expressly: their individual and specific histories meant that certain traditions were proper to the local churches under their bishops—traditions which, despite their partial character, enjoyed a unique title, and which must neither be overlooked nor abrogated—precisely in order that unity of the whole Church may exist.

[12] Sozomen, HE, VII, 19. 1, 2; cf. 19. 12 (GCS 50, ed. J. Bidez and G. Ch. Hansen, 1960, pp. 330 and 332).

Translated by John Griffiths

Adalbert Davids

One or None: Cyprian on the Church and Tradition

MORE has been preserved of Cyprian's correspondence than of that of any other Church Father before the First Council of Nicaea. In addition, many of his treatises testify to his deep pastoral care.[1] He was a bishop for less than ten years (249–258), but during this time Carthage became more and more the centre of the African Church. Two episodes stand out during his troubled episcopate.[2] During the persecution of Decius (250–251), when Cyprian fled from Carthage, there was a serious conflict—opponents received *lapsi* too readily into the Church again and *confessores* and *martyres* were very active in providing recommendations on the basis of which *lapsi* could be received back into the Church. Cyprian, however, was less lenient, and genuine solicitude both for the *lapsi* and for the *confessores* prompted him to warn against a too speedy reception into the Church. A group of his opponents organized their own community in Carthage, and a schism resulted. Cyprian elaborated his idea of the Church

[1] Cyprian's works were published by G. Hartel in *Corp. script. eccl. lat.*, III, 1–3 (Vienna, 1868–1871). For his letters I have used L. Bayard, *Saint Cyprien—Correspondance*, two vols., Collection Budé (Paris, ²1961–1962). For a bibliography, see B. Altaner and A. Stuiber, *Patrologie* (Freiburg, ⁷1966), pp. 172–81. I was not able to consult W. Simonis, *Ecclesia visibilis et invisibilis. Untersuchungen zur Ekklesiologie und Sakramentenlehre in der afrikanischen Tradition von Cyprian bis Augustinus* (Frankfurt a.M., 1970).

[2] See J. Lebreton and J. Zeiller, *De la fin du 2e siècle à la paix constantinienne*, Fliche-Martin 2 (Paris, 1946), pp. 186–210; K. Baus, *Von der Urgemeinde zur frühchristlichen Grosskirche*, Handbuch der Kirchengeschichte, 1 (Freiburg, ³1965), pp. 289 ff., 373–6, 401–406.

in the treatise *De ecclesiae catholicae unitate* (hereafter referred to as *De un.*).[3] After Bishop Fabian's death as a martyr, another schism came about in Rome: when Cornelius was chosen to succeed Fabian, his rival Novatian formed his own church community, which very quickly began to exert a strong missionary influence.

The first questions began to be asked in 255 about heretical baptism and it became clear that there were serious differences of opinion between Carthage and Rome.[4] The Bishop of Rome, Stephen, declared that only penance and the imposition of hands were required for Christians who had been baptized in heresy or in a schism. Cyprian, on the other hand, pleaded in favour of the North African tradition, according to which baptism was administered to converts of this type. All the North African bishops followed Cyprian, who was also supported outside his own territorial frontiers. Stephen threatened excommunication, but died suddenly in 257. Cyprian himself accomplished his *agon*, as he often called martyrdom, on 14 September 258, during the Emperor Valentinian's persecution.

I. Cyprian's Idea of the Church

De un. is the first treatise to deal explicitly with the Church. Throughout his life, Cyprian remained faithful to his declarations in this treatise against the schism and in favour of the unity or indivisibility of the local church. In brief, he maintained that, if there could be only one Church, there could only be one leader, the authentic bishop. Joint consultation (*consilium*), unanimity (*unanimitas*) and peace (*quies*) prevailed in this one Church. Heresy and schism, which were, for Cyprian, synonymous, were of the devil and the worst sin of all was to set oneself up in one's own "Church" in opposition to the one Church of Christ.

[3] I have used here the new edition of M. Bévenot, *The Tradition of Manuscripts. A Study in the Transmission of St Cyprian's Treatises* (Oxford, 1961), pp. 96–123. I have also referred especially to M. Bévenot, *St Cyprian. The Lapsed. The Unity of the Catholic Church*, Ancient Christian Writings, 25 (Westminster, Maryland and London, 1957).

[4] See H. Kirchner, "Der Ketzertaufstreit zwischen Karthago und Rom und seine Konsequenzen für die Frage nach den Grenzen der Kirche", in *Zeitschrift für Kirchengeschichte*, 81 (1970), pp. 290–307.

Everything that could be said about the Antichrist was applicable to a schismatic church. Cyprian took many examples from the Old and New Testaments to support, in *De un.* and his letters, the statement for which he has become famous—*Salus extra ecclesiam non est* (*Ep.* 73, 21, 2; cf. also *De un.* 6).

How did Cyprian arrive at this exclusive idea of the Church? The answer to this question is given especially in chapters 4 and 5 of *De un.*[5] Cyprian wanted, in a *compendium veritatis*, to set out the original, evangelical doctrine (*veritatis origo, caput, De un.* 3). Episcopal power was originally given, Cyprian argued, to one person, Peter. Later, Christ also allowed the other apostles to share in this *potestas*. Peter's *primatus* therefore enjoyed an historical priority over that of the other apostles. There could be no question of any authority over the other apostles (see *Ep.* 33, 1, 1; 73, 7, 1).[6]

Cyprian also saw the Church as part of the eternal *unitas* of God, the divine persons being one (John 10. 30; 1 John 5. 8). This

---

[5] The dating and traditional forms of these chapters constitute a very complicated problem. There are two main texts, called by Bévenot PT (Primary Text) and TR (*Textus Receptus*). Most scholars believe that Cyprian originally wrote PT, but replaced it at the time of the controversy about heretical baptism by TR, since Stephen is assumed to have used the text of Matt. 16. 18–19, which occurs in PT, to prove a juridical primacy of Rome over the other churches. *Primatus Petro datur* and *cathedram Petri* do not occur in TR. See especially O. Perler, "De catholicae ecclesiae unitate, cap. 4–5. Die ursprünglichen Texte, ihre Überlieferung, ihre Datierung", in *Römische Quartalschrift*, 44 (1936), pp. 151–168; M. Bévenot, *St Cyprian's De unitate Chap. IV in the Light of the Manuscripts*, Analecta Gregoriana 11 (Rome, 1937). For a rather more modified view, see J. Ludwig, *Die Primatworte Mt 16. 18, 19 in der altkirchlichen Exegese*, Neutestamentliche Abhandlungen 19, 4 (Münster, 1952), pp. 20–36; J. le Moyne, "Saint Cyprien est-il bien l'auteur de la rédaction brève du *De unitate* chapitre 4?", in *Revue bénédictine* 63 (1953), pp. 70–115, and M. Bévenot's refutation of this view, "*Primatus Petro datur*. St Cyprian on the Papacy", in *The Journal of Theological Studies*, n.s. 5 (1954), pp. 19–35; A. Demoustier, "Épiscopat et union à Rome selon saint Cyprien", in *Recherches de science religieuse* 52 (1964), pp. 337–69, especially pp. 359–67. P. de Labriolle, "Saint Cyprien. De l'unité de l'Église catholique", *Unam Sanctam* 9 (Paris, 1942), which contains a translation of PT and TR on p. 9, is misleading, because the first two sentences of chap. 5 belong only to TR, not to PT. Both texts are given alongside one another in Bévenot's *The Tradition*, pp. 99–101.

[6] See M. Bévenot, "Épiscopat et primauté chez saint Cyprien", in *Ephemerides Theologicae Lovanienses* 42 (1966), pp. 176–95.

unity, the source of the Church's indivisibility, was, he believed, continued in the Church, in Peter, in the apostles, in the bishop, in the college of bishops (*De un.* 6; see also *De dom. or.* 30, CSEL III, 1, p. 289, 6 ff.), the unity of the Church coming from above (*De un.* 7). However much the Church might be extended and develop, it still remained allied to its origin.[7] Cyprian illustrates this by three images (*De un.* 5), the same as those used by Tertullian to demonstrate the unity of the divine substance— the sun and its rays, the power of the root and the branches of the tree and the one source with many rivers flowing from it.[8] Cyprian could therefore say, with Tertullian, that the churches come from the apostles, the apostles from Christ and Christ comes from God (Tertullian, *De praescr.*, 21, 4; *Sourc. chrét.* 46, p. 114, 14 ff.).

Cyprian was dependent on Tertullian, but placed more emphasis on the bishop. His view of the Church was sociologically more accurate—for him, the one bishop in each Church was the only possible successor of Peter and the apostles. A "Church of the Spirit" of the kind defended by Tertullian at the end of his life was claimed by Cyprian for the concrete community gathered round the lawful bishop.[9] There could be no second bishop in addition to the lawful bishop—there could be none at all (*Ep.* 55, 8, 5) and a man such as Novatian, who opposed the one Church, *de facto* placed himself outside the evangelical and apostolic tradition by looking for the origin, not in God, but in

[7] See Tertullian, *De praescr.* 20, 7 (SC 46, p. 113, 25 ff.): "Omne genus ad originem suam censeatur necesse est. Itaque tot ac tantae ecclesiae una est illa ab apostolis prima, ex qua omnes. Sic omnes primae et omnes apostolicae, dum una omnes. Probant unitatem communicatio pacis et appellatio fraternitatis et contesseratio hospitalitatis. Quae iura non alia ratio regit quam eiusdem sacramenti una traditio." See J. Moingt, *Théologie trinitaire de Tertullien* 3, *Théologie* 70 (Paris, 1966), p. 984; see also Tertullian, *ibid.*, 29 (p. 125 f.) and *De bapt.*, 15, 1 (SC 35, p. 87, 11-12).

[8] Tertullian, *Adv. Praxean* 8 (*Corp. Christ., ser. lat.* 2, p. 1167 ff.). See also A. Demoustier, "L'ontologie de l'Église selon saint Cyprien", in *Recherches de science religieuse* 52 (1964), pp. 554-88, especially pp. 573-578.

[9] See H. Freiherr von Campenhausen, *Kirchliches Amt und geistliche Vollmacht in den ersten drei Jahrhunderten*, Beiträge zur historischen Theologie 14 (Tübingen, ²1963), p. 312.

himself.[10] For as long as Rome and Carthage continued to take the same attitude to the reception of *lapsi* and to the incipient schism, Cyprian's thesis concerning the indivisibility of the Church and the unanimity of the episcopate could be upheld without difficulty.[11]

II. IS THE BAPTISM OF NON-CATHOLICS A BAPTISM?

Cyprian was, however, very hard pressed when the conflict about "heretical baptism" broke loose. How was he to maintain his theory, which was based on mutual harmony in the local church and on collegiality of the bishops, when one of the leaders of the Church presumed to impose a local tradition on the other churches? Non-Catholic baptism was recognized in Rome. Following the Roman bishop Stephen, the traditional practices were maintained in the reception of converts—the imposition of hands was regarded as sufficient and even separated Christians did not rebaptize.[12] The baptism, on conversion to the Catholic Church, of Christians already baptized in another Church, was practised in Carthage and in other churches.

Cyprian had included baptism in his theory of *unitas*—any other than Catholic baptism was not (genuine) baptism, but a

---

[10] *Ep.* 69, 3, 2: "Novatianus in ecclesia non est nec episcopus conputari potest, qui evangelica et apostolica traditione contempta nemini succedens a se ipso ortus est"; *Ep.* 69, 5, 1: "[Novatianus] nemini succedens et a se ipse incipiens"; *Ep.* 69, 8, 3: schismatics set up their own *cathedra* and their own *primatus*; *Ep.* 45, 1, 2: the schismatic bishop is "adulterum et contrarium caput extra ecclesiam"; *Ep.* 55, 24, 1: "(Novatianus) Christianus non est"; *Ep.* 55, 24, 2: Novatian's Church is "*post* Dei Traditionem", it is only a "*humana* ecclesia" and its order is based on "*recentia* fundamenta"; cf. *De un.* 12: "haeresis et schismata *postmodum* nata" and Tertullian, *De praescr.* 29 (SC 46, pp. 125–6).

[11] The formula used by converted followers of Novatian, quoted by Cornelius, is interesting in this context: "... Nec enim ignoramus unum Deum esse et unum Christum esse Dominum quem confessi sumus, unum Sanctum Spiritum, unum episcopum in catholica esse debere" (*Ep.* 49, 2, 4); see also Cornelius' letter to Fabius of Antioch, Eusebius, *Hist. eccl.*, 6, 43, 11 (SC 41, p. 156).

[12] *Ep.* 74, 1, 2: "Si qui ergo a quacumque haeresi venient ad nos, nihil innivetur nisi quod traditum est, ut manus illis imponatur in poenitentiam, cum ipsi haeretici proprie alterutrum ad se venientes non baptizent, sed communicent tantum"; cf. Eusebius, *Hist. eccl.* 7, 2–3 (SC 41, pp. 167–8).

defilement (*De un.* 11; see also *De un.* 4; for the origin of the phrase, see *De hab. virg.* 19, CSEL III, 1, p. 201, 5 ff.). It was, Cyprian believed, not possible to speak of rebaptism in the case of converts—what they had already received was not a baptism at all (*Ep.* 71, 2–3; 73, 1, 2; 73, 24, 1). A letter by Bishop Firmilian of Caesarea to Cyprian has been preserved in Cyprian's correspondence, and it is clear from this that Firmilian supported him in his dispute with Rome; he appealed to Eph. 4. 5 (*Ep.* 75, 24, 3), whereas the Romans had used the argument of the "one baptism" (*Ep.* 71, 1, 3). Both sides, Rome and Carthage, appealed to tradition. Cyprian was able to use as an argument against Rome the fact that, ever since a council held under Bishop Agrippinus in Carthage (*c.* 225), the African Church had condemned heretical baptism (*Ep.* 71, 4, 1; 73, 3, 1; cf. Tertullian, *De bapt.* 15, SC 35, p. 87 f.). Firmilian of Caesarea (*Ep.* 75, 7, 5; 75, 19, 4) and Dionysius of Alexandria (Eusebius, *Hist. eccl.* 7, 5, 5; SC 41, p. 169 f.; 7, 7, 5, p. 172) also mentions other councils held in the East about that time at which the same decision was taken. Cyprian also maintained that local differences could certainly exist in church practices (*Ep.* 55, 21; cf. 72, 3, 1).[13]

Cyprian used other arguments—his North African tradition was on the right side, the only right side, that of *ratio*, of *veritas* and of the biblical tradition. Stephen's *consuetudo* could not be reconciled with Scripture (*Ep.* 74). The practice of Carthage was allied to the *origo*, whereas the Roman practice was simply a *humana traditio* (*Ep.* 74, 3, 1). In the light of Cyprian's view of tradition, this is a hard judgment. But Firmilian went even further than Cyprian, claiming that Stephen was excommunicating himself by his dictatorial behaviour (*Ep.* 75, 24, 2; cf. Cyprian's introduction to the council in the Autumn of 256, *Sententiae*, CSEL III, 1, pp. 435–6). Above all, Cyprian could not permit Stephen to oppose the judgment of the three councils at Carthage (255–6), which had approved his policy. Impressive *acta* of the last of these councils have been preserved; one of those present supported Cyprian with the words: "Christ said, 'I am the *veritas*'. He did not say, 'I am the *consuetudo*'. The *consuetudo*

---

[13] *Ep.* 55, 21; cf. 72, 3, 1 and M. Bévenot, "A Bishop is Responsible to God Alone (St Cyprian)", in *Recherches de science religieuse* 29 (1951–1952, Mélanges Jules Lebreton 1), pp. 397–415.

must yield to the *veritas*!'" (*Sententiae* 30, CSEL III, 1, p. 448, 4 ff.).

Neither side had strong arguments based on Scripture and, in the light of later developments, it is clear that Cyprian was also a loser. All the same, in opposition to the incipient schism, he evolved a theory of the Church which was bound to fail because of its exclusivity as soon as a successor of Peter, even though recognized as such by Cyprian, or by another leader in the Church, began to behave in a dictatorial way towards other local churches (*Ep.* 71, 3; cf. *Ep.* 30 of Novatian, 1, 2), and when the collegial government of his province was frustrated.[14] Stephen died suddenly in 257, but Cyprian did not apparently come into conflict with his successor Sixtus.

Augustine tried to exonerate Cyprian—the Donatists appealed to his theory—of all suspicion.[15] Certainly, as far as the great politicians of the Church were concerned, an entirely different view of the Church prevailed in the post-Nicaean period. According to Augustine (*De bapt.* 2, 4, 5, CSEL 51, p. 179, 13–17), a general council of the Church could have given a judgment in the event of such a difference, and Cyprian would have submitted to it.

[14] See J. Colson, *L'Épiscopat catholique. Collégialité et primauté dans les trois premiers siècles de l'Église,* Unam Sanctam 43 (Paris, 1963), pp. 103 ff.
[15] See especially J. P. Brisson, *Autonomisme et christianisme dans l'Afrique romaine de Septime Sévère à l'invasion vandale* (Paris, 1958), pp. 123 ff.

Translated by David Smith

Hervé-Marie Legrand

The Revaluation of Local Churches: Some Theological Implications

I. A Central Issue in the Post-Conciliar Reforms

THE subject of local churches is at the centre of the institutional and cultural crisis in the Catholic Church. This is a direct result of the ecclesiological reorientation of the last Council, which tried to revalue the episcopal ministry.

1. *The Council's Empirical Procedure*

After Vatican I, the Catholic Church had come to appear more and more as a single enormous diocese, the Pope's, within which the bishops were administrative assistants.[1] We all know that Vatican II decided to give episcopal conferences real power in order to check this centralization and to encourage collaboration between the bishops of the same region. These practical measures were of course the result of theological discussion, but because of the almost total absence of any Catholic thinking about local churches before the Council, working out a complete theology of the local church was never even considered, and the collegiality of bishops was often discussed without any explicit

---

[1] Maximos IV's intervention at the Council was revealing. "Some of the 'faculties' which it is proposed to 'delegate' to bishops make one wonder ... the faculty to allow one's priests to say two or three Masses a day, to allow one's nuns to wash corporals, purificators and palls *prima quoque ablutione*. Really, if a successor of the apostles cannot on his own authority allow nuns to wash purificators, what can he do? The lengths to which the theory of the Pope as the source of all authority in the Church has gone show how much it needs drastic revision if we are ever to get a sound ecclesiology."

reference to the collegiality of churches. It was therefore mainly by empirical means, such as the reinforcement of episcopal conferences and the formation of a synod to assist the Pope, that the image we had had until then of a "super-church" was discarded.

2. Relevance Today

The majority of Council Fathers expected the practice of collegiality to give them more freedom in their relations with Rome. But how many clearly wanted to move from the ideal of a single Church uniformly *Roman* everywhere to the model implied by the new practice, that of a communion of local churches presided over by the church of Rome, itself a local church? But, with the disappearance of Rome as an excuse, what had until then been concealed was now revealed, namely, that within the Catholic Church there is very little life in the local churches. The miserable progress made so far in increasing the importance of the bishops thus reveals a task of unsuspected magnitude. The reforms required, which are interrelated, have hardly begun. We shall list them in more detail.

3. Relations among Local Churches, and between them and Rome

The most obvious reform, if not the most important, concerns the relations between the local churches and Rome. Rome no longer has an official monopoly of initiative and has to make more and more decisions in consultation with other churches. The attitude of the many bishops' conferences at the time of *Humanae Vitae* or on the subject of priestly celibacy is sufficient evidence of the break with the past. The re-opening of the question of collegiality at the 1969 synod was a sign of the tension, which reappeared with the draft *Lex Ecclesiae Fundamentalis* (1971). From the ecumenical point of view, there would seem to be hope in this for a reconciliation with the Orthodox.

Nevertheless, it would be short-sighted, in my opinion, to consider only this aspect of the present evolution. The development of horizontal relations between churches is just as important for the future. Missionary solidarity with the young churches (the priests of *Fidei Donum*), the challenge to the churches of the West from those of the Third World on international justice, the demonstration of solidarity with the Brazilian church, and so on, offer many examples to show the existence, not of a united front against Rome, but of a growing inter-responsibility among the churches. But has this reciprocity between the churches, which will eventually include the Roman church, yet been given its proper place in our ecclesiology?

4. The Crisis within the Local Churches

The reciprocity I have just referred to presupposes vigorous local churches. But hasn't the local church virtually disappeared? Where is it to be found? In grass-roots communities? In parishes? Parishes are losing momentum. They are select groups, and hardly ever form a total environment. In the diocese? That is often, in Cardinal Marty's words, "an administrative federation of parishes". The picture presented by the diocese of Rome is a good illustration of this general decline in communal life: "The Church in Rome is not clearly seen as a community of believers but more as an institution embedded in society and responsible for worship and other religious activities. The link established between the Church and the 'faithful' is similar to that which exists between a public institution and its 'clients'."[2] The roots of this disintegration of the local church are as much sociological as theological, but is it not clear that both the identification of the Church with the clergy, which makes the laity irrelevant and isolates the ministers, and the restriction of the Church's mission to worship instead of the whole of social life, have a single cause, namely the absence of a theology of the Holy Spirit? A theology of the community cannot be separated from such a theology.

5. Local Churches are alien to their World

Particular churches have difficulty in being present to their world, that is to the social and political situation or culture. This is understandable in the case of young churches, but isn't it also true of the centres of Western civilization that the churches are becoming less and less indigenous? Signs of this are the irrelevance of their preaching and ethical teaching, their inability to

[2] Results of a sociological investigation sponsored by Cardinal Dell'Acqua, *La Documentation Catholique* 68 (1971), p. 94.

be a source of criticism of society, and the archaic life-style imposed on their ministers.

If the first two crises affect the internal organization of the Church, the last directly hinders its main task. It has been said time and again since Vatican II that the Church is for the world. How can this threefold challenge be accepted without further efforts to give life to local churches? I wish to emphasize three aspects of this proposal: (*a*) it is demanded by fidelity to Scripture and the Fathers; (*b*) it presupposes a more correct emphasis on a number of theological topics, as well as (*c*) a new look at the bishop's role as a unifying factor in the Church.

II. The Nature and Vocation of the Local Churches

1. *The Spirit calls the Church to remake what Babel constantly unmakes*[3]

The Church of the Fathers recognized its model in those "men from every nation under heaven" who gave thanks on the day of Pentecost for the good news, which each of them heard in his own language (Acts 2. 5–11). It saw this text as the Spirit's call to remake what Babel is constantly unmaking by taking all languages into its unity. And in fact the history of the Church, in this respect the history of exegesis, a composite of many cultures taken up by the force of Pentecost, has given birth to so many particular churches, Syriac, Greek, Latin, Armenian, Coptic, Ethiopian, Indian (Malabar).

Dogmatically, this means that the Spirit gives the Church a unity which can absorb differences without obliterating them and a universality which is always concrete, since the Spirit is the principle of both identity and difference. When the relation of the Church to the Spirit is forgotten, unity is replaced by uniformity; the dispute between the Indian and Chinese rites was settled by an order that worship in Peking and Benares should be in Latin, as in Rome—Babel rejected but not reversed.

But today we are gradually rediscovering the original meaning of the importance of the Spirit. Vatican II explicitly adopted the image of the reversal of Babel as the principle of its mission,[4]

[3] This idea is treated in greater depth in H.-M. Legrand, "Inverser Babel, mission de l'Eglise", *Spiritus* 11 (1970), pp. 323–46.

[4] *Ad Gentes*, 4.

and Paul VI told the Kampala Symposium, "You can and must have an African Christianity".[5]

We should therefore regard the theology of particular churches primarily as *coming under the heading of the relations between the Church and the world* (*or civilization*), and only secondarily as part of the theology of ministry. A diocesan church which does no more than reproduce the Church of another time or place is not particular, and is not fulfilling its vocation in the Spirit.

2. *The Local Church is fully the Church of God*

Far from being a part, and still further from being an administrative unit of the universal Church, the local church is the full presence and manifestation of the Church of Christ. Nothing in the New Testament allows us to make a distinction between churches in a house, in a town and in a region; they are all the Church. Similarly, a particular church never appears as part of a whole which possesses the fullness; the images of the body and the members or of the head and the members always refer to the relation between Christ and the Church, never to the relations of churches among themselves, or to that of the local church to the universal Church.

As it drew to a close in 1965, Vatican II gave, in *Christus Dominus*, 11, following on *Lumen Gentium*, 26, a definition of a local church which agrees with the New Testament: "Adhering ... to its pastor and gathered together by him in the Holy Spirit through the Gospel and the Eucharist, this portion constitutes a particular church in which the one, holy, catholic and apostolic Church of Christ is present and operative." Where the Spirit is, where the Gospel is, where the Eucharist is, where the apostolic tradition is, there is the Church. We may say with Louis Bouyer: "The Church does not exist all at once as a vast, universal system; on the contrary, it proceeds from essentially local communities and, strictly speaking, has no real existence outside these."[6] This excludes any administrative, numerical or exclusively legal concept of the unity of the Church.

---

[5] *La Documentation Catholique* 66 (1969), p. 765.
[6] Louis Bouyer, *L'Eglise de Dieu* (Paris, 1970), pp. 336–7.

3. The Local Church is not the Whole Church

Whereas it is wholly the Church, the local church would betray its vocation if it turned in upon itself, since each church is brought into existence by the Spirit to help in remaking what Babel constantly unmakes. As the Church's principle of identity and difference, the Spirit recognizes the Spirit and continually urges each church to restore communication between men and to establish communion between the churches.

There are also structural reasons why no apostolic church can turn in on itself. Its apostolicity has to be attested (or *transmitted*), it has to be received, always from outside—though the fact that the witness is outside the community does not mean that he is also external to the testimony. The basis of this structure of tradition and acceptance is the succession of episcopal ordinations. According to canon law, no bishop may ordain his own successor, nor may a community ordain its own bishop.[7] Since the First Council of Nicaea (325), which followed an older tradition, it has been an established rule that "the ordination of a bishop is the responsibility of all the bishops of the province", and a minimum of three are required to be present. Their presence and action bear witness to the identity in faith and apostolic ministry between the church in which the ordination is taking place and the churches from which they come, in other words the unity of the apostolic Church extended in space and time. By their action this identity is solemnly manifested, recognized and accepted, and the new bishop will thereafter be its irrefutable witness. Ordination must therefore be seen as connected with witness, and is much more the concern of the Church than of the individual.

The task which the bishop thus receives of both representing the Church in his church and his church among the other churches makes him a unifying factor in the Church, and bears witness to the reciprocity existing between the churches, each of

[7] The most recent studies show that Alexandria, which seemed to be an exception to this rule, was not in fact so. Cf. J. Lecuyer, "La succession des évêques d'Alexandrie aux premiers siècles", *Bull. Litt. Eccl.* 70 (1969), pp. 81–99; and L. Ott, *Handbuch der Dogmengeschichte* IV/5 (Freiburg–Basle–Vienna, 1969), p. 16 f.

which is actively responsible for the vitality of the one, Catholic and Apostolic Church.

4. *A Territorial Basis is not Part of the Definition of a Particular Church*

As we have seen, we must give a definite priority to human rather than to territorial regions in the definition of a particular church. Nevertheless, the territorial organization of the Church does have a meaning for ecclesiology. The amazing institutional continuity which has maintained into our own times both the special position of the bishop (since the time of Ignatius of Antioch?) and the territorial basis of the diocese (since Nicaea II in 787?) is a means of guaranteeing the catholicity of the Church. If the Church were organized on some other principle than that of territory—by race, social class or language—it would probably be more like a club whose members elected each other.[8]

In Western urban civilization, parishes and dioceses still have the task of overthrowing the power of Babel and giving substance to catholicity. Not by being communities—that would be a sociological illusion—*but by permitting communication between groups*, whether Christian or not. However essential grass-roots communities (because of their freedom to choose their members), or parishes based on a shared language or common worship, may be, they need the experience of the people God has gathered together, in all its normal diversity, with its conflicts of language, race and economic interests. Nor should they stop short of confrontation.

III. New Emphases and Directions in the Theology of Particular Churches

1. *The Church of Christ is also the Church of the Spirit*

The process by which a universally uniform clerical institution has almost replaced the communion of churches has complex historical and sociological causes. I shall restrict myself here to a theological explanation. It was implied above that the main

---

[8] For an historical and theological study of the territorial basis of dioceses, see H.-M. Legrand, "La délimitation des diocèses", in *La Charge pastorale des évêques, Unam Sanctam*, 74 (Paris, 1969), pp. 177–219.

theological cause was the "Christomonism" of the medieval
Latin tradition. In that context it was normal for the relation of
the Church to Christ to be seen as that between an association
and its founder. The founder left his powers to the apostles,
who passed them on to the hierarchy. Therefore the internal
unity of the community broke, for a non-reciprocal relationship
was set up between the ministers and the community (governors
and governed, teachers and taught). For this reason the hierarchy came to identify itself with the Church, by making all
the decisions for it, by drawing new members from a closed
circle (and refusing to allow elections), and by trying to eliminate,
even in principle, any control by the community over ministers
or teaching. It was a logical evolution. But the effect on the
trinitarian balance of our life in the Church resulted in the disintegration of all elements of community. It also affected relations between the churches and between the Church and the
world.

The loss of the idea of the gift of the Spirit as the principle of
unity and difference brought a rigid uniformity into the conception of life in the Church—the identity of the terms "Catholic" and "Roman" in some languages is significant! But, as
Dombois has said, the unitary Church cannot be the type of
the unity of the Church; and we must draw the conclusions of
this position for ecumenism.

Finally, by presenting itself as an institution overwhelmingly
dominated by the clergy, the Church is polarized by its liturgical
activity, and is incapable of serving and challenging society as
it is required to do by the Spirit of Christ, which was given to
it to enable it to carry on the work of judging the world which
Jesus began (cf. the gospel of John). The rediscovery of the importance of the Spirit can now be seen as the key to the revival
of particular churches. I shall summarize the other new emphases
which follow from this. Even if they are sometimes strange, it
will be evident that they are part of the authentic tradition.

2. Theologically, the Particularity of a Church stems from its Relation to the World

This has been its vocation since Pentecost: every nation heard
the *same* good news and gave thanks in its own language. There

has to be more than one encounter between the good news and social, political and cultural reality; it is in these spheres that attentiveness and response meet to produce the salvation which a people can then proclaim. A local church should not try to be different for the sake of difference, but it cannot reproduce a hypothetical universal Church; its task is to be its presence. The relative failure of the liturgical reform as a universal translation of the Roman rite is surely an indication that this sort of imitation is no solution. Even in a particular place the Church must do more. Repetition does not ensure authenticity; that requires creativity.

3. Collegiality not primarily between Bishops but between Churches

The emphasis at Vatican II was more on the collegiality of bishops than on that of churches, even though in the final texts it is not possible to separate the two and give priority to the collegiality of bishops.[9] Much is involved in such a shift of emphasis, because taking the collegiality of churches as a function of that of bishops makes it impossible to see the ministry as service, dissociates it constitutionally from the community, and encourages a false universal and legalistic conception of the Church. In contrast, the structure of transmission and acceptance which is the mark of apostolicity requires the bishop to be in the Church and the Church in the bishop. If the Church is often so little in the bishop today, is this not because the bishop is no longer in the Church? A recovery of the proper balance requires (a) an immediate reform of the procedure for appointing bishops to include at least a consultation with the churches concerned, (b) the abolition of formal ordinations (in the case of cardinals, nuncios and members of the Curia), and above all (c) a new look at the basic charismatic structure of the Church, in which all have received the Spirit for the common good.

4. Primacy in the Church belongs to a Particular Church, the Church of Rome, whose Bishop is the Pope

This follows from what has been said above. If the college of bishops is above the Church, and not an organic part of it, this

---

[9] See my analysis in "Rôle de l'évêque et nature de l'Eglise", in *La Charge Pastorale des évêques, op. cit.*, pp. 103–21.

must *a fortiori* be true of the Pope. He is Christ's vicar over the universal Church; what additional significance can there be in his ministry in the diocese of Rome? The *Annuario Pontificio* puts the diocese of Rome in an appendix, as if by succeeding Peter the Pope only secondarily became Bishop of Rome. Yet it is by becoming Bishop of Rome that the Pope becomes Pope. This was the accepted view until recent times, and it follows from the reciprocity between the bishop and the Church (does not traditional usage talk as much of the *sedes* as of the *sedens*?), which is based on a theology of the Spirit. Vatican I did not change this, nor did it transform the Bishop of Rome into a bishop of the Catholic Church. This title, with which Paul VI signed the conciliar decrees, in fact means that he is bishop not *of* but *in* the Church.[10]

Fidelity to the tradition is, in this respect, the guarantee of a Church which is one and diverse, and directly of unity with the Orthodox. It also implies criticisms of some recent suggestions:

(*a*) There is no more reason to want the Pope to be elected by the bishops than to want the bishops to be elected by the Pope. This is to reverse the system without escaping from a false universality which prevents the Church from being a communion of churches.

(*b*) It is normal for the Pope to be an Italian—after all, he is the Bishop of Rome. Of course, if the Pope were everything and the other churches nothing, it would be necessary to fight against what would be an unjustifiable national monopoly.

(*c*) In the long run would it not be better to involve the Romans in the choice of their bishop? There would be other *de iure* participants, bishops of neighbouring churches, in the spirit of tradition and acceptance—and of course Rome has a large neighbourhood!

5. *There is Reciprocity between the Churches*

The reciprocity of local churches is based on the apostolic structure of tradition and acceptance. Even more, because of the fundamental charismatic structure of the Church, the totality of

[10] H. Marot, "Note sur l'expression 'Episcopus catholicae Ecclesiae' ", *Irénikon* 37 (1964), pp. 221-6.

the gifts of the Spirit is to be found only in the totality of the Church. No particular church can therefore claim to have a monopoly of them which allows it to dominate the others, or to be so far above them that it need not be interested in their faith or their situation. The *raison d'être* of each church obliges them all to collaborate, and to be concerned for each other and—collectively—for unity. This is the basis of horizontal relations between churches. The dangers inherent in the national character of episcopal conferences make it necessary to develop multinational and continental structures, and to preserve the primacy, which is a gift of the Spirit to the Church. The primacy will then take its place, under the influence of the growing *affectus collegialis*, within the reciprocity of communion as service to the particular vocation of each church. This will also calm legalistic suspicions and anxieties, and is necessary at a time when the ecumenical movement is beginning to discover the importance a primacy will have within the universal Church of the future.

IV. The Rediscovery of the Bishop as the Unifying Factor in the Church

Within his own church, the bishop is the bond and guarantee of unity. But just when the local churches are coming to life again, and to further the process, we must rediscover that even more central feature of his ministry, written into it at his ordination, which makes him the link between his church and the whole Church, and vice versa. And the new view must avoid giving priority to either side of the relationship; the fundamental assumption is that the bishop is in the Church and the Church in the bishop.

The bishop must be in the Church. What Augustine said of his ministry, "A bishop for *you*, a Christian with *you*", must be made a reality in structures. How can a bishop represent his church if he is not a part of it, if he is not constantly attentive to it? And he must go further, and encourage Christian freedom. When a bishop puts himself forward as an official in authority he loses his authority and shows himself incapable of helping his church forward into the future—and that is his task. If the bishop wants to be part of his church, he must accept conflicts with other churches (or with certain groups). One bishop has already said, "Living in communion does not consist in living without tensions, or pretending that they don't exist. One is not living in communion if one irons out diversity and suppresses questions."[11]

The Church must be in the bishop. Must not the Church remain in contact with the bishop, who, for it, is a witness to the whole Church? "To watch over the Catholic faith received from the apostles", to see that after being damaged by a false universality his church does not shut itself up in a false particularity, to keep it attentive to "what the Spirit says to the churches", to stimulate the spirit and reality of communion with other churches, is surely what is required of one who is the bond of unity in the Church.

The decisive steps taken at Vatican II require bishops to be more than ever the bond of unity within the Church. They also require us to place the collegiality of bishops firmly in the context of the collegiality of churches.

[11] Mgr Coffy (Bishop of Gap), in *Communautés nouvelles*, June 1970, p. 45.

Translated by Francis McDonagh

Leonardus Meulenberg

Gregory VII and the Bishops: Centralization of Power?

DE MAISTRE, putting his case for the Pope, persists in having a dig at Voltaire. Especially, whenever occasion arose, for being so tough on the figure of Gregory VII. What, after all, can compare with this proud moment, the Emperor *en route* for Canossa? And yet Voltaire dares call him a fool, who added the Church to the roll of the saints, just as the peoples of antiquity elevated their protectors to the status of gods. But whatever wise and sensible folk may think, there is no refuting a fool: *"il suffit de le présenter et de le laisser dire!"*[1] This radically divergent posture is but a single item in the age-old controversy centred upon the figure of Gregory VII. He has been a perpetual symbol of contrariety, right up to our own day. And not without justification: his character had such a quality of *élan* about it that it was bound to cause dissension and divide opinion. On this point all are agreed.

Plenty of attention has already been lavished on the problems arising out of the complex struggles between the spiritual and temporal powers. It was under Gregory VII that they first came to a head. Here I intend to confine myself to the claims advanced by Gregory VII internally, within the Church. I realize, of course, that "within the Church" is an inept expression in this context; but it is the best one for describing the object of my present inquiry. In this area, too, a number of writers have already been active; but for the most part they have touched on the theme only in passing.

[1] J. de Maistre, *Du Pape* (Antwerp, 1820), p. 219, note 1.

Furthermore, I hope in what follows to demonstrate that their point of view frequently calls for some finer distinctions to be drawn. Most of them are agreed that Gregory VII set out deliberately to weaken the hierarchical organization of the Church to the advantage of a rigid, tightly knit papal authority. Thus also Knowles, whose manual on medieval church history appeared recently in Dutch. Knowles remarks that the centralization of power which was based on Gregory's conviction that he had a universal authority and at the same time bore a universal responsibility, took many forms. Where the hierarchy was concerned, Gregory VII reduced the importance of the regional primacy to a minimum; he reduced the powers of an archbishop to the job of consecrating his suffragans and presiding over synods, while the diocesan bishops came under the immediate supervision of Rome.[2] That there are some grains of truth hidden in this observation nobody is going to deny. But is that all there is to be said?

I. TRADITION

"We are returning to the decrees and doctrine of the holy Fathers, we are importing nothing new, nothing that we ourselves have invented."[3] Anyone wanting to be fair to Gregory will not allow himself to brush these words aside as a non-committal platitude. The Pope reiterates them too often for that. It therefore becomes important to examine briefly what the basis, the root, of this tradition is for Gregory. After all, if we can to some extent specify the sources, this should give us a criterion for checking the Pope's thinking and behaviour against the actual character of the ideas currently obtaining.

In particular, it is a matter of finding out which canonical texts were circulating in curial quarters at the time. Now, thanks

---

[2] M. D. Knowles, *The Church in the Middle Ages—The Christian Centuries*, Vol. II (London, 1969).

[3] "Ad sanctorum patrum decreta, doctrinamque recurrimus nihil adinventione nostra statuentes, sed primam et unicam ecclesiasticae disciplinae regulam et tritam sanctorum viam relicto errore repetendam et sectandam esse censuimus", *Registrum III*, 10, ed. E. Caspar, MG. Epp. Selectae (Berlin, 1920–23), p. 266.

to the research done by J. Ryan and A. Michel[4] we know that Peter Damiani relies primarily on the *Dionysio-Hadriana* and Burckhardt of Worms' decretal, but Humbert makes use almost exclusively of the Pseudo-Isidorian Decretals. Moreover, both reformers were probably familiar with the writings of Auxilius and Vulgarius. In addition, however, there is the fact that partly under Hildebrand's influence the most diligent search was made at the time in the Roman archives for documents that might substantiate the Pope's claims. Which of them have since been lost, we do not know. At all events we have the collections of Anselm of Lucca, Bonizo of Sutri and Deusdedit. We can take it, though, that their opinions were for a great part known to the Pope. Whatever the discoveries made later on, in those days it was these collections which embodied the tradition. Especially as far as the Pseudo-Isidorian Decretals were concerned. They represented then the authentic tradition of early Christianity.

So we are faced with some richly variegated material that Gregory could possibly have used. But if anyone expects to find clear references in his letters, then he is sorely mistaken. The one thing we know for certain is that the Pope used the Pseudo-Isidorian Decretals as assembled by Humbert in the *Diversorum Sententiae Patrum*. Without excluding the influence of other sources, this is therefore our principal touchstone. For the rest, it goes without saying that we must also take into consideration the ideas of the reformers themselves.

Broadly speaking, my intention now is to bring out certain aspects of Gregory's thought and activity that shed light on just one side of his nature. These are things which in my view are all too often lost sight of. In their wake the question arises as to how these aspects fit in with Gregory's behaviour as a whole. Without committing myself finally on this, I do really believe that the traditional picture will have to be presented at any rate in very much greater depth.

---

[4] J. J. Ryan, *St. Peter Damiani and his Canonical Sources. A Preliminary Study in the Antecedents of the Gregorian Reform*, in Pontifical Institute of Medieval Studies, Studies and Texts (Toronto, 1956); A. Michel, "Die Sentenzen des Kardinals Humbert, das Erste Rechtsbuch der Päpstlichen Reform", in *Schriften des Reichsinstituts für ältere Deutsche Geschichtskunde* (Stuttgart, 1952).

II. Vicarius Petri

On what does Gregory base his claims? With all the emphasis
he can muster he pushes the Roman church to the fore. It is the
"mother of all the faithful", the "mother of all churches".[5] This
last is given particularly powerful emphasis. Thus the Pope
writes to Gregory, the Catholicos (Patriarch) of Armenia, that
the Roman church "on the authority of St Peter, by way of privilege has since the very beginning been designated by the holy
Fathers the mother of all churches and so will ever be regarded
as such".[6] This special position goes back to the apostles Peter and
Paul, "by whom the Roman church was established in Christ".[7]
Above all, however, to Peter. It is "his church".[8] To him "as the
first one" Christ gave the power to bind and to loose, in an "ex-
ceptional way" the Lord entrusted to him the care of his sheep.
And "by a special grace" he is given to understand: "I have
prayed for your faith."[9] Thus it can astonish no one that in the
Dictatus Papae Gregory affirms "that the Roman church has
been founded by the Lord alone".[10] Rather, it is remarkable that
this extremely important datum is adduced only here.

As head of the Roman church Gregory bears the title, in particular, of "vicar (representative) of the apostles"[11] and most of
all, "vicar of Peter".[12] Here we find the basis for his interpretation of the papal primacy. "Jesus Christ", he writes, "appointed
St Peter to be chief of the apostles, by giving him the keys of the
kingdom of heaven and the power to bind and loose, both in
heaven and on earth. Upon him he also founded his Church,
with the command to tend his sheep. Since then this dignity and

[5] *Reg.* V, 13, Caspar, p. 366.
[6] "Per Beatum Petrum quasi quodam privilegio ab ipsis fidei primordiis
a sanctis patribus omnium mater ecclesiarum astruitur et ita usque in
finem semper habebitur" (*Reg.* VIII, 1, Caspar, p. 513).
[7] "Romanae ecclesiae ordinem et officium recipiatis, non Toletanae vel
cuiuslibet aliae, sed istius, quae a Petro et Paulo supra firmam petram per
Christum fundata est et sanguine consecrata" (*Reg.* I, 64, Caspar, p. 93).
[8] *Reg.* III, 6, Caspar, pp. 253-4.
[9] *Reg.* II, 70, Caspar, p. 230; *Reg.* I, 15, Caspar, p. 24; *Reg.* II, 31, Caspar,
p. 167.
[10] "Quod Romana ecclesia a solo Domino sit fundata" (*Reg.* II, 55a 1,
Caspar, p. 202).
[11] *Reg.* IX, 14, Caspar, p. 593.
[12] *Reg.* I, 68, Caspar, p. 99.

power have been passed on by St Peter to all who take his seat or will do so to the end of the world. This is a divine privilege and right of succession."[13] It is one of the few occasions on which Gregory gives a sharper definition to his position as Bishop of Rome. He rapidly brings together the most important texts from the gospels and then draws a line of connection between the papal authority and that of Peter: every bishop who mounts his seat thereby shares in his privileges as well. It is an important point that Gregory is plainly emphasizing here the official nature or aspect of his position. As "Peter's deputy" he stands in the long succession of Roman bishops who had exercised their authority in the seat of the chief of the apostles. The import and substance of this authority derive from the texts concerning Peter in Matthew and John. Luke alone is lacking in this respect. But elsewhere Gregory says clearly enough: "The apostolic seat, which without any merit on our side we occupy by divine dispensation, under his guidance from the beginning has not succumbed and will remain inviolate under his protection, since the same Lord testifies: I have prayed for you...."[14]

III. VICARIUS CHRISTI

But how do things stand with the other churches and with their leaders, the bishops? Certainly, Gregory's assertion that the Roman church is the mother of all churches is most emphatic. But beyond that he leaves this idea to be worked out in more detail. It had in fact already been done. Not only do the *Diversorum Sententiae Patrum* underline Gregory's claims; they also carry a passage by Pseudo-Vigilius, which is very important in this connection. "It is beyond doubt that the Roman church is the foundation of all churches and bears their destiny within

[13] "Jesus Christus beatum Petrum constituit principem apostolorum dans ei claves regni coelorum et potestatem ligandi et solvendi in coelo et in terra; super quem eciam ecclesiam suam edificavit commendans ei oves suas pascendas. Ex quo tempore principatus ille et potestas per beatum Petrum successit omnibus suam cathedram suscipientibus vel usque in finem mundi suscepturis divino privilegio et iure hereditario" (*Reg.* IX, 35, Caspar, pp. 622–3).
[14] "Apostolica enim sedes, cui quamvis immeriti Deo auctore presidemus, ipso gubernante firma permansit ab ipsis primordiis eoque tuente illibata permanebit testante eodem Domino..." (*Reg.* III, 18, Caspar, p. 284).

itself. Every true believer knows, after all, that from it all churches take their origin." Thus the passage. It derives from Innocent I, who upheld it with respect to the churches in the West. Now it is turned into a general pronouncement. Pseudo-Vigilius goes further: "This church, which is the chief one, has so transferred its deputizing function to the rest of the churches that they are called to a share of its concerns, but not to the full-ness of its power."[15] The text this time goes back to Leo the Great, who addressed himself in such terms to his representative in Thessalonica. The allusion here is to a limited delegation, to rights which Rome, as the primary see in the West, liked to call her own. Now, however, it sounds as though all churches rest solely on the representative function they exercise in the name of the Roman church. The later reformers, in any case, think in just the same way.

That Gregory does not take over these ideas is the more sur-prising when we see that he made regular use of the "deputizing" concept. But without exception those cases are concerned with some special task or responsibility of the Roman church, an instruction addressed either to its legates or to bishops charged with settling this, that or the other piece of business. A particular case is the way in which Gregory tells the Corsicans to accord the Bishop of Pisa, as the Pope's representative, the same honours "as ac-cording to the ordinance of the Fathers should be done to those whom the Holy and Apostolic See wishes to have a share in its solicitude".[16] Perhaps there is an allusion here to the passage cited from Leo the Great's letter. But not as with Pseudo-Vigilius. The point at issue here is the transfer of the special rights that the Roman church had long exercised over Corsica. And in this Gregory is in line with his illustrious predecessor. Beyond that, he has no wish to overstep the proper limits. On the contrary,

[15] "Nulli dubium est, quod ecclesia Romana fundamentum et sors sit ecclesiarum, a qua omnes ecclesias principium sumpsisse nemo recte creden-tium ignorat. . . . Ipsa namque ecclesia, quae prima est, reliquis ecclesiis vices suas credidit largiendas, ut in partem vocatae sint sollicitudinis, non in plenitudinem potestatis", D.S.P. 12, ed. P. Hinschius, Decretales Pseudo-isidorianae, et Capitula Angilramni (Leipzig, 1863), p. 712.

[16] "Qualem ex constitutione patrum his exhiberi oportet, quos sancta et apostolica sedes in partem suae sollicitudinis assumendos esse praevidet" (Reg. V, 2, Caspar, p. 350).

his aim is "in all things to revive the good repute of the churches which the Lord by his blood has made his own".[17] Although Gregory springs to the defence of the honour of Rome, he at the same time wants to recognize the peculiar and inalienable rights of the other churches. Like Peter, other saints have their "see" to watch over. It is occupied by the bishops. In their church they are the pastors, who must treat the faithful with the greatest respect. A bishop enjoys "the rights springing from his authoritative office".[18] And that office has been instituted by the Lord; nay more, he lives in the bishop. This is put in surprisingly clearcut terms when Gregory learns that the people of Carthage have denounced their bishop to the ruling power, the Saracens, and that as a result he has been thrown into gaol and maltreated. "O wicked example, that disgraces you and the whole holy Church! Once more Christ is made a prisoner, is judged by false accusers and witneses, is counted among thieves and beaten with rods!"[19] The bishop is the representative of Christ. The inhabitants of Arles must remember, therefore, that they can live in peace only if there is someone "who leads the way for them in Christ's stead and protects them from the snares of their wily enemy".[20] And when the growth of church leadership in Poland leaves much to be desired, Gregory makes the point that "after God, the Christian religion and its ordering depend *par excellence* on those who are the shepherds and governors of Christ's flock".[21]

---

[17] "Ut exaltationem ecclesiarum, quas etiam Dominus noster suo proprio sanguine acquisivit, in omnibus sublevare et melius restaurare possimus" ("Privilege of the church of Bologna", ed. L. Santifaller, *Quellen und Forschungen zum Urkunden- und Kanzlei-Wesen Gregors VII: I Quellen, Urkunden, Regesten, Facsimilia*; Vatican City, 1957, p. 50). Although the Roman church has been founded by the Lord alone—the charge to Peter that he should go from Antioch to Rome—the others have likewise been called into being by him, albeit through the agency of human beings.

[18] *Reg.* II, 45, Caspar, p. 183.

[19] "O exemplum iniquum, vestri et universae sanctae ecclesiae dedecoris exemplum. Christus iterum capitur, falsis accusatoribus et testibus condemnatur, inter latrones numeratus verberibus caeditur" (*Reg.* I, 22, Caspar, p. 38).

[20] "Nisi qui eius vice vobis presit et contra incursus callidi insidiatoris ... vos muniat, habeatis" (*Reg.* VI, 21, Caspar, p. 433).

[21] "Christianae religionis ordo et provida dispensatio ab his permaxime post Deum pendit, qui Dominici gregis pastores et rectores esse videntur" (*Reg.* II, 73, Caspar, p. 234).

But what then is the relationship between the Pope and the rest of the bishops? Gregory sees them as "brothers" who together with him are bound to protect the flock. Deplorable conditions in the Church are therefore to be laid primarily at the door of the bishops, Gregory included. "We are the root and cause of such an evil, we who have been chosen to govern the people and commissioned for the salvation of souls."[22] Ought they not to enter the lists for the Lord? "For it must surely put us to shame", Gregory writes to Siegfried of Mainz, "that day by day any number of knights do battle for their prince, defying mortal danger, and we who are called the priests of the Lord, we would not engage in warfare for our king?"[23]

Having reached this point, it will be worth our while to hear what some of Gregory's contemporaries have to say—especially in view of those last words. The image that Gregory employs here is also made to bear a different interpretation: namely, that in the Pope the bishops are to acknowledge their king. Hence Humbert adduces against Cerularius a privilege of Constantine in which the latter gives the Pope of Rome an undertaking that "all bishops shall accept him as their chief, as judges do their king".[24] This idea goes back via Aeneas of Paris to the *Acta silvestri*. Indeed, it is not just Humbert who is familiar with it. Among later reformers we find a certain Bernold of Constance who unblushingly declares that the Pope enjoys the same kind of authority as a king who, although he may divide his kingdom among various dukes and knights, in no way abandons his complete authority.[25] Gregory, however, does not agree with this. He

[22] "Verum huius tanti mali nos caput et causa sumus, qui ad regendum populum prelati et pro lucrandis animabus episcopi vocati et constituti sumus" (*Reg.* II, 45, Caspar, p. 183).

[23] "Multum namque debet nobis videri pudendum, quod quilibet seculares milites cotidie pro terreno principe suo in acie consistunt et necis perferre discrimini vix expavescunt, et nos, qui sacerdotes Domini dicimur non pro illo nostro rege pugnemus" (*Reg.* III, 4, Caspar, p. 250).

[24] "Privilegio, quod idem princeps quarto baptismatis sui die devotus contulit pontifici Romano, scilicet, ut in toto orbe sacerdotes ita hunc caput habeant, sicut omnes iudices regem" (*Epistula I ad Cerullarium*, c. 10, ed. C. Will, *Acta et Scripta, quae de controversiis Ecclesiae Graecae et Latinae saeculo undecimo composita extant*, Leipzig, 1861, p. 70b).

[25] "Quilibet episcopus nec super gregem sibi commissam tantam potestatem habeat, quantum presul apostolicus, qui licet curam suam in singulos episcopos diviserit, nullomodo tamen se ipsum sua universali potestate

adheres to the title which the Pseudo-Isidorian Decretals assign to a bishop. He is the representative, the vicar, of Christ.

IV. THE MYSTIC

We have now acquainted ourselves in broad outline with the background. But how did Gregory set out to make the privileges of the Roman church a reality? It is on *this* score that he has been most keenly criticized. Does he not create the impression that for the Roman church he, Gregory, is the sole source of guidance; that the whole of Christendom should bow to his will? Here we are faced with an aspect of the Pope's personality that needs some clarification: his almost mystical love for Peter, his master, his father. This man had nurtured Gregory in the faith from his earliest childhood and had then chosen him to govern the Church. But now the Pope is greatly troubled and oppressed. He is afraid that if Jesus does not take up the reins of government with Peter, he will succumb. The world is, after all, imbued with the presence of the Evil One. Satan rules! In these straits Gregory turns again to Peter for assurance. More than that. He identifies himself with Peter in a mystic surrender. Thus the two parties to a dispute are to conclude a lasting peace in pledge to St Peter and to himself, so to speak. And the faithful are commended when in Gregory's exhortations they hear the voice of Peter himself; for it is through the Pope that Peter speaks. The letters Gregory receives hold no mysteries for him. It is Peter who lays bare the real intentions of the writers. Over all who try to suborn the Pope hangs the fate of Simon the Sorcerer. In short, it is for every Christian to realize that in the person of Gregory, Peter is honoured; and wrong done to Gregory is done to Peter. Such a mystic bond entails, however, that the importance attaching to the Pope is considerably accentuated. Through Gregory one can put the omnipotent bearer of the keys under obligation. Even here on earth he showers his venerators with benefits. Everyone is well advised, therefore, to give their complete backing to each and every desire or enterprise of Gregory's. In it all

---

privavit, sicut nec rex suam regalem potentiam diminuit, licet regnum suum in diversos duces comites sive iudices diviserit" (*Apologeticus*, c. 23, ed. M.G.Lib. de Lite II; Berlin, 1891, pp. 87–8).

the honour of Peter is ever present to the Pope's mind. And he flies into a fierce rage if ever his master's rights are endangered. Those concerned set at risk their bond with Peter and the Pope. On the other hand, Gregory goes to a lot of personal trouble to show favour to the loyal devotees of Peter. Indeed, what strikes us most forcibly is Gregory's firm belief that each pope is sanctified, is rendered holy, by the merits of Peter. This notion does not appear only in the *Dictatus Papae*, but plays a part in Gregory's thinking as a whole. It is something he knows from personal experience, as he himself says.[26] What are we to make of all this? A. Nitschke[27] sees in Gregory's mysticism the dominant thing that casts everything else into the shade. In our view, however, a distinction has to be drawn. Nobody is going to question the fact that in this is rooted the great driving force by which the Pope was actuated. It is another thing, however, whether Gregory really made this personal piety of his apply in areas where he found himself confronted by a substantial and solid tradition; in other words, whether he completely overlooked the official aspect of his position as Bishop of Rome.

V. Concern for a Sound, Hierarchical Structure

Without going into every controversial issue—the scope of this article does not permit that—I should like to pick on a number of aspects which at any rate may give us food for thought. For instance, whenever it becomes an issue, ensuring the free election of bishops. For the Pope it is beyond question that the shepherd must enter the sheepfold by the door, that is, Christ. And his voice is heard in the choice exercised by clergy and people. Thus one of the major accusations levelled against Rainer of Orleans is that by all accounts he "has wormed his way into the Church, contrary to the decrees of the Fathers, without having been duly selected by the clergy and people".[28] After that, the candidate has to be consecrated by three bishops of the province.

[26] *Reg.* VIII, 21, Caspar, p. 561.
[27] A. Nitschke, *Die Wirksamkeit Gottes in der Welt Gregors VII. Eine Untersuchung über die religiösen Äusserungen und politischen Handlungen des Papstes* (Studi Gregoriani, V; Rome, 1956, pp. 115-219).
[28] "Dicitur ... contra decreta sanctorum patrum sine idonea cleri et populi electione ecclesiam invasisse" (*Reg.* V, 8, Caspar, p. 358).

That results from the organic independence which every church must have, including the church in Africa, where Archbishop Cyriacus of Carthage has only one suffragan. Gregory counsels him to have a third candidate elected and to send him to Rome for consecration, "so that you yourself will be in a position to consecrate bishops, as the sacred laws prescribe".[29] The metropolitan is to superintend these consecrations; and he must see to it that the choice made is fair and above board. The Pope stresses this when exhorting Humbert of Lyons "to let nothing deter him from having the elected bishop—Landri of Mâcon—consecrated either by himself or by his suffragans, at any rate if it can be shown that the authority of the Fathers presents no obstacle".[30] Accordingly, Gregory is ready to act on a complaint lodged by Manasses against his suffragans of Laôn and Soissons, who "without informing you and asking your advice" have consecrated the candidate from Amiens.[31] We even know of a case where the Pope refuses to consecrate a bishop for Miletus because he has been given to understand that it was the right of the church of Reggio-Calabria to do this. "Therefore", he writes to Roger of Sicily, "I consider myself unable to accede to your request, unless after careful inquiry it transpires for certain that the consecration is not a prerogative of the church of Reggio."[32] It is also Gregory's desire that the bishop should receive full recognition in his role as shepherd. At diocesan synods the bishops may call anyone to account; and the Pope persistently urges them to exert their authority. He also wants to see this maintained over against the rest of the bishops. Nobody has the right, outside his own diocese, to dismiss clergy or reinstate them in their office. And when it comes to ordination, Gregory himself points out to the

[29] "Quatenus . . . a nobis ordinato vobisque remisso necessitati ecclesiarum ut sancti canones precipiunt episcoporum ordinationibus succurrere valeatis" (*Reg.* III, 19, Caspar, p. 285).

[30] "Ut fraternitas tua neque gratia alicuius dimittat, quin electum (Landri of Mâcon) . . . episcopum seu per te seu per suffraganeos tuos ordinare studeat, si tamen auctoritas sanctorum patrum probatur sibi non obviare" (*Reg.* I, 36, Caspar, p. 58).

[31] *Reg.* VI, 2, Caspar, p. 394.

[32] "Under non aliter annuendum postulationi tuae perpendimus, nisi diligenter examinata iustitia Melitensem ecclesiam ad prefatae Regitanae parroecchiae consecrationem non attinere constiterit" (*Reg.* IX, 2, 25, Caspar, p. 608).

man anxious to become a priest that he must approach his own bishop for that. Then the latter should investigate the candidate's character and conduct.[33] Thus in his diocese the bishop is the one who represents authority; and this calls for obedience. Gregory frequently returns to this point. Even if the bishop is wrong, the faithful are not relieved of their obligation. To rebel against him is therefore a criminal act. In this connection, the Pope at the same time refers to the authority of the martyrs Fabian and Stephen.[34] It is the only place where Gregory is evidently making use of the *Diversorum Sententiae Patrum*. But the other ideas are likewise strongly emphasized in that collection.

However, as soon as we move on to the question of provincial church order, things are different. Admittedly, even the *Diversorum Sententiae Patrum* allows the metropolitan the right to consecrate his suffragans. But beyond that he possesses hardly any power at all; for any differences that occur must be settled "by common agreement". And no one may be left out of the discussion. The further point is then made that any metropolitan who acts contrary to this risks being deposed—and his actions are null and void.[35] Nothing at all is said about a measure of obedience on the part of the suffragans. With a background of this sort, in complete conformity with the line taken by the Pseudo-Isidorian Decretals, Gregory could have undermined the metropolitan's authority altogether.

In fact the Pope took a different course. "More especially", he writes to Boleslaw of Poland, "we must attend to the fact that the bishops of your country, since they have no fixed metropolitan see, are under no authority, roam around at pleasure and adopt a freer posture than the decrees of the Fathers provide for".[36] Such a see is necessary in order to structure Christendom within a given area. It is ordinations that Gregory has primarily in view. But in addition there are the provincial councils, to

---

[33] *Reg.* II, 61, Caspar, p. 216.
[34] *Reg.* VII, 2, Caspar, p. 461.
[35] *D.S.P.* 65, 90, 192, Hinschius, 724, 502, 139.
[36] "Illud nobis primum attendendum est, quod episcopi terrae vestrae non habentes certum metropolitanae sedis locum nec sub aliquo positi magisterio huc et illuc pro sua quisque ordinatione vagantes ultra regulas et decreta sanctorum patrum liberi sunt et absoluti" (*Reg.* II, 73, Caspar, p. 234).

which the Pope gives considerable prominence. Here the bishops can stand up for their entitlements. Here they must render account. Thus Theodoric of Verdun, who believes that he has been hard done by. And Isembert, the firebrand of Poitiers, who is arraigned at Rome. In this last case it is expressly stipulated that the Archbishop, Gosselin of Bordeaux, conduct the inquiry.[37] Furthermore, Gregory sees in such provincial councils the organ appropriate for ensuring that reform could take firm root. That is why he advises Anno of Cologne to convene a council for that purpose.[38] That such occasions provided the metropolitan with no merely theoretical authority we may deduce from other things that Gregory says. He requires obedience from the suffragans. Rebellion is not to be tolerated; but then the reverse is equally true. According to the Pope, Siegfried of Mainz should have intervened in the quarrel between Jaromir of Prague and John of Olmütz long before. That is "a lax interpretation of his office".[39] The same message reaches the ears of Manasses of Rheims, who has persistently failed to proceed against Roger of Châlons for illegally dispossessing his clergy of church property.[40] In short, we see Gregory accentuating the authority of the metropolitan.

Besides the metropolitans we find in the *Diversorum Sententiae Patrum* yet a third agency: the primates. This body is an invention of the Pseudo-Isidorian Decretals. The primates form a court of appeal for the suffragans; but their authority is purely passive. They are allowed to mediate only if requested to do so. To mediate—that is all. For if the accused maintains his innocence, there is nothing anyone can do.[41] It is a further means of screening off the suffragans. Through the primates the power of the metropolitans is to be curtailed from above, without enabling the primates to become a danger in their turn. But which sees have the right to a primacy? The *Diversorum Sententiae Patrum* points us solely to the vicariate of Arles, as consolidated by Gregory the Great.[42]

The Pope also speaks of this: namely, when Manasses appeals

[37] *Reg.* I, 81, Caspar, p. 116; *Reg.* I, 73, Caspar, p. 105.
[38] *Reg.* II, 67, Caspar, p. 224.
[39] *Reg.* I, 60, Caspar, p. 88.
[40] *Reg.* II, 56, Caspar, p. 204.
[41] *D.S.P.* 73, 84, 99; Hinschius, 201, 131, 473.
[42] *D.S.P.* 235, Gregorius I, *Reg.* XI, 56, M.G.Epp. II, Berlin 1891, p. 337.

against him to privileges which give Rheims too the primacy. As against that Gregory argues that Arles had likewise received such privileges. All the same, Rome had later ceased to confirm them. Privileges are not a ground for action in law; they are a favour.[43] But then we are amazed to behold the Pope, scarcely a year later, inducting Gebuinus of Lyons into the primacy over the provinces of Rouen, Tours and Sens. In so doing he is pleased to restore the old division which the Popes had taken over from the civil rulers. With them the head of the provinces had been a magistrate. In an ecclesiastical context this became the primate, who thus obtained control over the metropolitans. So it was with his illustrious predecessor, Anacletus.[44] Gregory bases himself in this on the ideas of the Pseudo-Isidorian Decretals. As H. Fuhrmann has shown,[45] we find there a view about the primates essentially different from the one that underlies everything we know up to and including Sens. Here the plan is based on the *Notitia Galliarum*; and it presents a clear, sharply defined division, the consequence of which is that like the metropolitan the primate can support his status by reason of the local see that he occupies. As opposed to the privileges we know so well, we have here an organic stage in the hierarchical order, not a personal concession corresponding more or less to existing political boundaries. But in the belief that it had to do with procedures initiated by the Fathers, Gregory made a reality for the first time out of the discovery of the Pseudo-Isidorian Decretals. Futhermore, in the Pope's case we perceive few of the restrictions that gave something of a hollow centre to the primatial authority. The metropolitans of Rouen, Tours and Sens owe the church of Lyons the same sort of respect their suffragans owe them.[46]

All this serves to show that Gregory's intention is not simply to recognize the bishops as "representatives of Christ". He also aims to affirm and reinforce the hierarchical sector as such.

[43] *Reg.* VI, 2, Caspar, p. 393.
[44] *Reg.* VI, 34–5, Caspar, pp. 447–52.
[45] H. Fuhrmann, *Studien zur Geschichte mittelalterlicher Patriarchate II* (Z.R.G. 71, Kan. Abt. XL), 1954, pp. 14–35.
[46] *Reg.* VI, 35, Caspar, pp. 450–2.

Translated by Hubert Hoskyns

Alois Müller

Obedience to the Bishop

ALL parties in the Church are anxious to include the question of authority in any discussion of the role of the bishop. On the one hand there is a somewhat admonitory or nervous insistence on the authority which the bishop must have "all the same" because..., and on the other there is a negative fixation on the subject and a willingness to consider in connection with the role of the bishop only such problems as the "structure of domination", repression, and so on. Hence a discussion of the bishop's function is still useful. The requirements of this journal indicate a discussion of the dogmatic question, and not primarily of the morality of command and obedience,[1] or a discussion in terms of canon law or pastoral theology.[2] We must try to find out what "obedience to the bishop" is in the light of what theology can tell us about the nature of his office. But our findings must be directly related to the contemporary situation in the hope of constructing a "practical theology of episcopal authority".

We must be careful to avoid any *a priori* approach to the dogmatic theology of the episcopal office. The precariousness, or at least diversity, of the biblical and historical bases for any precise delineation of the nature and functions of the "episcopate" are well known. This leads to the temptation to give, for purely theoretical reasons, exaggerated importance to a random principle,

[1] I have examined this topic in "Authority and Obedience in the Church", *Concilium*, Vol. 5, No. 2 (1966), pp. 40–8 (American edn., Vol. 15).
[2] Cf. N. Greinacher in *Handbuch der Pastoraltheologie*, Vol. 3 (Freiburg, 1968), pp. 93 ff., 103–10.

and to use it as a "stringent proof" of what one already regarded as likely—the classical procedure of every ideology. The only presuppositions which will be made in this article are the following: (*a*) The bishop is what he is today, the church official responsible for a diocese in virtue of his membership of the universal college of bishops. (*b*) In the course of these duties he carries out a part of "the apostolic office", which requires fresh examination by systematic theologians.

I. THE MEANING OF "OBEDIENCE TO THE BISHOP"

What has "obedience" to do with a bishop's exercise of authority in his diocese?

1. *Illumination and Legalism*

We can start from the Pseudo-Dionysian theory of illumination: as the highest vehicle of the Spirit, the bishop has a duty to "enlighten" all his subordinates, so that in general there can be no safer or smoother path for a cleric or a layman than obedience to his bishop.[3] In the West this idea has a predominantly legal stamp. The holder of an office is regarded as having the prerogative of leadership; as a result of this legal position, there is a duty of unconditional obedience to a legitimate incumbent. In both cases there is a duty of obedience derived directly and formally from the bishop's supernatural "title".

2. *The "Oath of Allegiance"*

At the end of the ceremony of ordination to the priesthood comes the ritual promise of obedience to the bishop: *Promittis mihi et successoribus meis reverentiam et oboedientiam? Promitto.* This ritual, first recorded at the end of the thirteenth century and officially adopted by Rome in 1596, goes back, as Jungmann has shown,[4] to an old High German "priest's oath" of the ninth century, which made the priest a kind of vassal to the

---

[3] This view is found as early as the third century in the *Didache*, chap. 15.

[4] J. A. Jungmann, "Das Gehorsamsversprechen nach der Priesterweihe und der althochdeutsche Priestereid", in *Universitas. Dienst an Wahrheit und Leben*, Festschrift für Bischof Dr. Albert Stohr, Vol. I (Mainz, 1960), pp. 430–5.

bishop, and bound him in particular to remain in the bishop's service and not to move to another diocese. In a time when it was not uncommon for bishops to be involved in political disputes, such an oath could draw priests into them; as early as the ninth century, we find synods objecting to the oath's being interpreted as setting up a feudal relationship.[5]

It is important to realize that the complex historical inheritance of the priest-bishop relationship contains not only mystical and theological components, but elements connected with civil law and even with politics. It is not surprising to find these features ignored or even obscured by assertions of a "supernatural basis", but there is also another danger. When a promise originally intended as a regulation of practice is later justified theologically, practice has the effect of inflating theology. The theology has to be given a higher value than it is worth, and we are faced once more with ideology. It is even legitimate to ask how far the pre-eminence in theology and law of episcopal authority is simply the result of the ideologization of the original element of feudal law.

3. *"Structures of Domination"*

Since the bishop-priest relationship included such "non-theological" quasi-feudal remnants, it is not surprising that they should have grounded a negative interpretation of the bishop's claim to obedience as simply one example of the structure of domination which has completely taken hold of the Church. On this view this claim can be justified on any other than theological grounds; it is a politico-cultural phenomenon, to be attacked in terms of a criticism of society; the Church is even seen as the starting-point for social change. It is easy to see that ideology is at work here, in a negative way; the theory that the episcopal office is simply a mode of domination was developed, not to justify existing practice, but to change it or to justify prejudices against it. The mistake is not the discovery of a dominative structure in the neo-Marxist sense in episcopal authority; the feudal legal survivals are already evidence of this. The mistake is made when the total phenomenon of episcopal authority is reduced to a dominative structure in society.

[5] Jungman, p. 432.

4. *The Structure of the Church as Theological Essence and Historical Development in Interaction*

Since the attempts we have mentioned to find the basis of the duty of obedience to the bishop have proved unsatisfactory or one-sided, we are left with the problem of interpreting this phenomenon.

(*a*) *Implications of the structure of the Church.* Today again we start from the Church existing in this local, or better, regional, grouping which is the diocese. Where the Church exists, it exists with the structure of the "apostolic office".[6] This given structure, the bishop's function and corresponding activities therefore form part of the Church as it is realized in practice.

(*b*) *Interaction of theological essence and historical development.* As conceived by theology, the "apostolic office" resists the objections made against it. It is "apostolic", which means it has to do with the Holy Spirit; but because it is an "office" it is an institution, and therefore necessarily a sociological phenomenon. Its spiritual pedigree and social justification are both in turn attacked with equal force. Nevertheless, it is only when both are taken seriously that we can make a serious theological statement.

In ecclesiological offices theology, history and sociology exist in a *circumincessio*. It is as dangerous to theologize social situations which are products of historical development as it is to deduce from *a priori* theological premises the social forms which should exist. Immediately the office enters the realm of human society its form is determined by historical conditions. This form, however, constantly refers back to the theological basis of the office and thereby creates among the members of the Church a particular consciousness of the office. This consciousness in its

---

[6] Cf. G. Hasenhüttl, "Das kirkliche Vorsteheramt. Seine Funktion und seine Entwicklung", *Wort und Wahrheit* 25 (1970), pp. 542-52; *id.*, *Charisma. Ordnungsprinzip der Kirche* (Freiburg, 1969). In my view, Hasenhüttl's theory (function = charisma, structural consolidation [in definite offices] = sociological epiphenomenon) does not agree with New Testament thinking, which I shall discuss below. The New Testament makes no distinction between theology and sociology (it is this distinction which gives theology its appearance of being fundamental), but sees the guidance of the Spirit *in* the (sociologically determined) situation of the Church.

turn, together with cultural influences, then has an effect on future historical and social developments within the Church.

It is impossible for us today to stand outside this process. We are faced with the sociological dimension of the office, which bears the marks both of the hierarchical and absolutist past and of the present-day trend towards democratization.[7] From the point of view of the sociology of the Church, the problem is to democratize an office with an absolutist structure.

We are also faced with the theological dimension of the office. This does not mean the fact that a bishop may *iure divino* inadequately represent to his church an inadequate institutional form. The theological dimension of the office means that the body of the Church cannot be reduced to the status of a human social organization, but has as its head the risen Lord. Everything to do with the Church is relative, which means that it refers back to the Lord; naturally this applies above all to the function of leadership in the Church. In both aspects, therefore, the function of leadership is connected with the Lord. When this reference to the Lord is made part of a system, which cannot be other than a human system, its inviolability is endangered, whether the system stresses Platonic illumination or Roman law. But the impossibility of fitting this transcendental reference of ecclesiastical office into a system does not mean that it can be ignored, still less that it can be quietly dropped. On the contrary, it gives a sharper form to our problem: how can we give effect to the reference back to the Lord in the particular social form taken by the office at a particular time? How can leadership be "democratic" without becoming disobedient to Christ? How can the office insist on obedience without measuring itself against the lordship of Christ? I shall now try to relate these theoretical questions to the present situation.

II. Practical Suggestions and Definitions

1. *Positive Implementation of the Structure*

If a diocesan church is to be "alive", and if it has an appropriate structure, of which the office of the bishop is part, it is

[7] Cf. *Concilium*, Vol. 3, No. 7 (1971) (American edn., Vol. 63).

clear that much of this "life" will depend on the bishop's directives and on the "obedience" of the members of the church.

(a) *The position of the bishop.* Our practice is still at the stage of implying that the bishop is the Church; we must therefore constantly insist that the bishop is an accountable leader *of the Church*, which is all of us. Nevertheless, there is one element which must not be overlooked in the new view, namely, that it is part of the bishop's responsibility as a member of the college of bishops to represent to his particular church the greater unity of the world Church and thereby to bring "the Church" to the attention of "his church". This relation between the local church and the world church must be seen dynamically. It is not always the case that only particular views predominate in the local church and universal views among the college of bishops; the position can be reversed, since the degree of adaptation to the universal norm, the will of Christ, may be greater in the local church than in the universal Church. In general, however, this is the area in which the bishop enjoys inalienable precedence in the diocesan church; a view held by the world Church and maintained by the bishop cannot be overruled by an opposite view in the local church, whatever form it takes. This is where the dynamic tendency towards ever greater unity has its effect; the "churchliness" of a particular local community is a function of its active participation in the greater, universal unity.

This law naturally admits of degrees. It has its full force in the confession by the community of the apostolic faith. Similarly with the desire for communion in structural unity (in peace and unity with the Apostolic See). The force of this general principle is lessened to the extent that it is applied in less important matters, and after a period of insistence on a blanket unity there is now a new awareness of the necessary distinctions. A bishop too must realize that it is his duty to observe these distinctions in representing the world Church, and not to insist on complete administrative uniformity.

If the local church's answer to the bishop's exercise of this function is called "obedience", the word should not be understood in a positivistic sense ("There is the rule—now obey it."). It is more than this; it is an acceptance of and attention to (*ob-audire*) the universal norm of what it is to be the Church, which is always in the background and of which the bishops are only representatives. The position is seriously misrepresented if one is willing to discuss such problems only as "authoritarian centralism".

Given this function of the bishop (we shall ignore particular questions of temporary local dissent in regard to secondary matters), he now has to fill the role of leader of a fraternal community. "Governing" here means more than giving orders and seeing that they are carried out; it means seeing that every element of the diocesan organization functions. Ways of forming consciousness, finding solutions to problems, decisions, explanations, feed-back (i.e., communication from "below" to "above"), all this is a life-process on many levels. In this process, orders have a function, and those who receive them should not react neurotically; equally, attention (*ob-audire*) to all objective and personal factors is as important a duty for the bishop as giving orders.

(*b*) *The position of the members of the diocese.* What was said in the last section in fact applies for the most part to the members of the diocese as well. They too are part of a complex organism in which they have a position to fill. But the word "obedience", which applies to a different and simpler organizational model, must be replaced by terms such as "interest" and "commitment" (which of course implies a tie as well as enthusiasm). A person who commits himself totally to the life of the diocesan church will certainly play his part. In such a situation many aspects of carrying out instructions from above will remain unchanged, but this "obedience" will be related primarily to an activity; it will be seen more as participation in an accepted totality, and less as personal submission to the individual will of one in authority. Whether this sort of relativism will also have the wrong kind of depersonalizing effect depends on the individual case; in general, however, it is the model which fits the situation.

But in this respect, is the *priest* in the same position as a member of the diocese who is not ordained? Has he not, precisely at his ordination, given a promise of obedience which, even purified of false interpretations, makes his position vis-à-vis the bishop more closely defined? We shall arrive at an answer to this question in stages.

We may say, firstly, that it is wrong to start positivistically from the promise and say: "The promise was made, therefore the priest is in such and such a relation to the bishop." When a particular interpretation of the promise cannot be related to the real or desirable situation it should be abandoned. On such grounds the promise was at a very early date freed from its association with feudal obligations.

We may also say that, *in general*, the priest stands in the same relation to the bishop as any other member of the diocese. This follows from a view of the diocesan church as a whole, and particularly today, when it is a long time since all the active and important participants in the life of the diocesan church were priests. And it would certainly be regarded as *male sonans* if we adopted the negative formulation: "Lay-people owe the bishop less reverence and obedience than priests."

Finally, we should remember that priests are "the bishop's presbyterium" from a sociological viewpoint too. Functionally, they relate more closely to him. The whole contemporary structure of the diocese could not function without a much closer functional relation between the priest and bishop than between the bishop and the ordinary layman. In matters of education, appointments, and church activity, the bishop must be able to exercise an immediate authority. At the same time the relaxation of social relations within the Church means that in questions of ordinary life, such as dress, individual life-style and political or social activity, the priest increasingly feels in the same position with regard to the bishop as any other member of the diocese. In this area it would only be an unnecessary exercise of legal and moral authority if a bishop tried to enforce an outdated interpretation of the duty of obedience.

A functional interpretation of priestly obedience does not mean that the concept is secularized, and that the bishop relates to the priest more as, say, a local government official. Sociological theory must make sociological sense, but as a whole it is taken up into the sphere of faith, where the Church is the body of Christ and every ecclesial encounter is an encounter with Christ. This means that the basic law of love, unity and peace must govern every relationship on both sides, and that, objectively, the building up of the body of Christ remains the unchanging common goal.

2. *Conflict and its Resolution*

It would be naïve, unhistorical and unbiblical to believe that within the framework I have described there could no longer be conflicts in the Church, particularly about "disobedience". Nor is the answer given by monastic spirituality any longer adequate; according to this, when there is a conflict "the subordinate must obey", and hope for a final solution of the problem from "bearing this cross". Not that this principle is to be despised, but it should not be used as an excuse for not trying to find the best possible human modes of relationship and relying on supernatural short-cuts.

The objective possibility of conflict exists because there is nothing to show that a bishop, in virtue of the grace of his office, will find the correct solution rather than impose a false one. The solution inspired by the Holy Spirit is often to be found in the Church, and it is the bishop's duty to accept it from there. In this context too there can be no theological short-cuts; all the resources of the natural sphere must be used, and faith in the supernatural dimension must operate within this totality.

Of course, it is often—again by human standards—anyone's guess what the results of an incomplete solution will be as compared with those of a conflict, and which choice is objectively justified. On the other hand, there must be an end to the (mainly "supernatural") dramatization of conflicts in the Church. Since there is already an article on this subject, it will be sufficient to refer to "the practical theology of settling conflicts".

Two complementary factors—confidence and control—are indispensable in this connection. Where there is no confidence in the good will, loyalty and faith of the other party, there can be no solution of the conflict, but only acrimonious dispute or the tyranny of whichever group proves stronger—a situation unworthy of the Church, whichever side exercises the tyranny. It is essential to accept that the other party also subjectively wants the Church's present mission to be carried out as effectively as possible.

But no one in the Church has an absolute claim to such confidence. Everyone must be aware both of his own limitations and of whatever competence the other party may possess. For this another factor must be introduced: control. This word can have an "unloving" sense, particularly in English and French, where it can mean restriction or even repression. It is intended here to mean mutual openness and the possibility of expressing an opposite view. It is common human experience that a person whose activity never encounters opposition from "control" or contradiction will invariably become one-sided in his views. Control, then, is a normal and necessary factor in the life of the Church, as elsewhere. Confidence and control must regulate the life of the diocese as they do that of the world Church. If opposing views are expressed, this should not be seen as implying a lack of confidence, and certainly should not be answered by a withdrawal of confidence on the other side. The difficulty of technical problems necessitates conflict. If it is borne in this spirit, the solution appropriate to the particular situation will somehow be found. An intolerant insistence on perfection on the one hand, and authoritarian impatience on the other, make a solution impossible—as so many examples at present show.

"Obedience to the bishop" means making the objectives of the diocesan church one's own and, in one's own place within the unity of the Church, doing everything possible to assist its mission. St Paul's advice applies to all: *Non plus sapere quam oportet sapere, sed sapere ad sobrietatem* (Rom. 12. 3).

Translated by Francis McDonagh

Ruud Huysmans

The Diocese as an Administrative Unit

A PROFOUND and eager longing possesses the Churches. Their structures, forms of organization and modes of government ought to witness to the unique character of this community as the people of God: "If leadership and friendship can be combined—as they were in the New Testament—then this combination should be very evident in the Church. Therefore we must develop models of leadership, both because the world needs to see these models and because our own tradition, especially as it is symbolized in the relationship between Jesus and his disciples, requires it of us. These models are much more important than our experimenting with ecclesial structures without any such models having been made available."[1]

"The Church may, therefore, perhaps be described as the 'paradigmatic institution'. It is to proclaim the aim of all institutional life, recognizing alienation as a deep existential crisis, which, however, cannot be thought of as a final fate of society, without hope for a rebirth grounded in the generating power of God, who for ever remains faithful to his covenant with mankind."[2]

In the project-report of the Dutch Pastoral Council, *Ideas and*

[1] A. W. Greeley, "Leiderschap in de kerk van de toekomst", *De toekomst van de kerk, verslagboek van het wereldcongres Concilium te Brussel*, p. 136.

[2] W. D. Marsch, "The concept of institution in the light of continental sociology and theology", *Institutionalism and Church Unity*, ed. N. Ehrenstrom and W. G. Muelder (London, 1963), p. 49.

Experience of Authority, this problem is posed as follows: "In the Church too there is obvious uneasiness about the exercise of authority.... That such unease should be felt more intensely within the Churches is evident enough when we remember that we are here dealing with a distinct type of personal community. The Church is, after all, *communio*, a brotherhood of all with one another in the Lord. This *communio* is the fundamental category for all relations within the Church."[3]

This affords a basis for the contention, warmly expressed, that so far as possible the structures of the Church be determined by its own unique character. Being what they are, the Churches must make real an experience of human community in which the tension between the institution and the person ceases to have a one-sided outcome. "We are no longer going to have just an ecclesiology of the institution but one that is capable of combining what persons are able to contribute with what has been 'institutionalized' and one in which diversity can be led in the direction of unity."[4]

This task, which at the same time entails a challenge, presents itself at all levels of a Church's life and is ecumenical, because the tendencies that set ecclesiastical authority outside the believing community can be a mark of any Church.

I. THE DIOCESE AND THE BISHOP

No one is going lightly to deny the connection adumbrated in such dictums as: where the bishop is, there is the Church; where the Church is, there is the bishop. To call that connection simply an ideal would be to impugn its value; yet to regard it as always self-evidently present does less than justice to the real state of affairs.

As soon as we try to make out what a bishopric, a diocese, is, a kind of tension arises. Vatican II restored to the diocese the old significance which it had been in danger of losing because of the preponderantly administrative character assigned to it in the

[3] *Pastoraal Concilie van de Nederlandse Kerkprovincie*, pub. Katholiek Archief, 1968, Pt. 2, p. 11.
[4] Y. Congar, "Wezenlijke structuren voor de kerk van morgen", *De toekomst van de kerk, op. cit.*, p. 142.

Latin Church; for it then appears as primarily a canonical institution, the object of a bishop's power of jurisdiction. What that
emphasizes very strongly is that the ecclesiastical status of what
happens in such an area of episcopal ministration is determined
by its connection with the bishop. To vary somewhat the words
of Cyprian, one might say, on the basis of this sort of approach:
whoever is not with the bishop is not with the Church.[5] The
"churchly" character of liturgy, words, actions and a whole
variety of initiatives is then derived, as it were, from the approval
or concurrence of the bishop. The bishop appears as the one by
whom the entity "diocese" is made to constitute "Church".[6]

Vatican II did not see the diocese primarily as an administrative unit, whether as an administrative or territorial subdivision
of the Church as a whole, or as a constituent part of the Church,
midway between universal Church and local church community.
Its concern was with the diocese as "a part of the people of God"
(populi Dei portio), gathered together into one in the Holy Spirit,
through Gospel and Eucharist. That is why the one Church of
Christ is present and operative in this specific and particular
ecclesial community.[7] In that context the bishop emerges as the
one who together with the priests is charged with making this
possible. Adopting this sort of approach may seem obvious enough,
provided it is not made in too facile a spirit; for when it comes
to what actually happens in a diocese, the emphasis is different.
Just as, according to this view of the matter, the "churchly character" of this part of God's people does not derive primarily from
the bishop, so too his approval or disapproval, his consent or dissent, in short, his decision, cannot of itself be held to determine
and confirm the aforesaid "churchly character". Such a line of
thinking is risky, because in a church still largely structured and
envisaged in different terms, it is in danger of being misunderstood. One may then come to be suspected of rejecting the "ver-
tical, paternal type of control" to "the exclusive advantage of a
norm based on the horizontal, fraternal principle". But instead

---

[5] Cf. Cyprian, Ep. 66, VIII, 1.
[6] Cf. H. C. Laan, De rooms-katholieke kerkorganisatie in Nederland
(Utrecht, 1967), pp. 173–234.
[7] Christus Dominus, no. 11: "populi Dei portio" replaces the words:
"Dominici gregis pars".

of dividing off the intermediary organs and authority-structures and developing them separately for their own sake, the intention is to set them back into the community as functional services.[8]

This is essential, if we want to avoid making the bishop and his pastoral mandate a fiction without any corresponding reality. That happens just the same if everything that takes place in a diocese is thought of as happening with him or with his authority, or if his approval at any rate is implicitly assumed, as making it "all right". The conversion of his apostolic mandate from fiction into reality becomes an odious business, if he is at variance with the course of events. His episcopal authority is then displayed in a purely negative way, because he is bound to obstruct this or that development. He is then the brake, the one to voice the reservation and take the eventually negative decision. Such a distortion of his mandate is a real danger, resting as it does on the exaggerated idea that everything happening in a diocese is made "ecclesial" by his explicit or putative approval.

With an interpretation which sets out to correct a view of the bishop that sees him as somehow separate from his diocese, a number of difficult questions assume a different aspect.

II. ADMINISTERING A DIOCESE—AND THE ADMINISTRATIVE CRISIS

Traditionally, the administration of a diocese was not an arduous job. After all, what there was to do by way of pastoral care, preaching, liturgy, catechism, mission, the training of priests, and the interpretation of theological points was more or less hard and fast. On the one hand the bishop would apply what was the universal rule or had been laid down by the Holy See in Rome, and on the other he would supplement this to some extent in accordance with his own insight or with local custom. In the executive process, problems of business and finance would arise, of course, along with personal questions relating to the clergy and laity. But it was a matter of giving guidance in accordance with settled terms. What his judgment determined was more or less law.

There are several reasons why all this has undergone a change. A plurality of opinions is on the increase; in not a few places

[8] Y. Congar, op. cit., p. 139.

there is a concentrated search for new forms; communication on a great variety of initiatives and ideas does not stop short at the frontiers of a diocese; theological insights are changing; and there is growing up a new, almost indefinable style of life in the Church. Whereas, in an earlier period, episcopal leadership was aimed primarily at applying what was universal and at the prevention and control of deviant and disturbing situations, a bishop's task today is to give guidance and direction to changes that are already taking place and have usually not been initiated by him at all. It is here that incontestable schemata simply let him down. There is neither time nor opportunity for him to keep an eye on everything himself. A whole number of things that are undergoing renewal—e.g., liturgy—can no longer be straightforwardly managed by the diocese. New forms of pastoral activity are needed, but at the same time are still in doubt. The need to lead and to guide in processes of change becomes the first priority.

To be an administrator, as people are now discovering, is no longer a matter of being able to appeal to authority in order to legitimize this or that decision. Administration takes up a lot of time and study and calls for consultation with the parties concerned, so that one may be enabled, with others, to formulate insights and reach a consensus. In two respects at least the bishop's traditional status as sole legislator in his diocese has been affected: from the side of the (usually national) bishops' conferences with their commissions and various study-agencies, and from the standpoint of the individual diocese where, at any rate on a regional basis, people are marking out lines of procedure for themselves. A changing Church brings with it a number of problems on a bigger scale than a diocese, while other questions are being resolved on a smaller scale, regionally or locally.

Even so, the authority of the bishop, his immediate colleagues and, where they exist, the episcopal offices is still considerable. Diocesan management is involved in many matters for many reasons, not least because it appoints and dismisses priests and must often have a decisive voice in the economic and financial side of things. None the less a change of course presents itself. Diocesan government may be reduced to the role of approving this and rejecting that. The theoretical strength of this kind of government, however, can become its material weakness; for it then continues to depend on the bishop's competency to decide. This disadvantage, reinforced by the fact that the diocese emerges as an authority remote from the church community, is still present when the diocesan curias are greatly expanded, with the result that the whole process of governing still very much resembles and suggests the capacity to take binding decisions. Or else one takes another way, more difficult because it is new. The situation in which the church community for a large part finds itself involved may be characterized as one of change, of searching for new forms, of pondering the old message, experimenting, giving shape to a new relation between Church and society. In this movement, expecting the diocesan government to be the more or less decisive authority and court of appeal with regard to all these developments is not realistic. In such circumstances the traditional mark of ecclesiastical government—namely, decision-making of a compulsory nature—is very much reduced in value. What this means, structurally speaking, is that the autonomous, more or less isolated position of the bishop and the diocesan curia vis-à-vis the diocese must be changed; for there is a correlation between the task an administrator is expected to fulfil and the structure within which he works.

III. The Diocesan Councils

It is here that the role of the diocesan pastoral and priests' councils may become valuable. It is possible to disagree about the historical and theological motives behind them. One may seek to examine to what extent they displace or have succeeded to more or less flagging and more ancient collegial organs in a diocese. There is a field for investigation regarding their number in each diocese and their relation to one another. But they have been introduced into the Church since Vatican II—and just when a more vital conception of the diocese was breaking through—of the diocese as "a part of the people of God"—and the bishop was being defined theologically less as the bearer of a power of jurisdiction than as a pastor. The cohesive relationship between these factors gets seriously upset when the incipient councils are greeted with the oft-repeated message that they have only an advisory and consultative competency, whereas the bishop retains his authority to decide. In a sense this is simply to give added strength to what one had intended to oppose. It may serve to make the situation in which a bishop or a diocesan curia find themselves more explicitly odious and bring them into a state of implicit isolation.

Without expecting too much of these councils, they are at the moment witness to the fact that a diocesan administration, which has to give a lead in various changes, does not have enough permanent partners in dialogue for the purpose. One can take it as read that where relations between the bishop and these councils are felt to be based in practice on the distinction between advice and decision-making, a major disappointment is going to ensue.

The old idea that "managing" is the same as autonomous decision-making will in that case persist. But there is a growing understanding in our society that discussion and consultation are not merely valuable forms of human intercourse but methods that make administration possible. Verbal formulation of what is really at issue in a given situation, exposing the contributory factors and working out new lines of action for the future call for discussion with other people. Authority is not thereby undermined, but on the contrary given substance and meaning. Surely, in a church, a community where the gifts of the Holy Spirit are to each and every person, it is not to one man but rather to many that the truth and the right way will be known.

In a church where other traditions have prevailed for so long it is not easy to give the councils a real task to perform. That this is bound up with the exercise of authority by the bishop and his curia cannot be denied. At the First Symposium of Bishops of Europe, held from 10 to 13 July 1967, at Noordwijkerhout (The Netherlands), these themes were linked with each other: authority and obedience in the church on the one hand, the priests' councils and pastoral councils on the other.[9] It is of vital importance to the functioning of these councils that the diocesan government should want discussion with them and should feel the necessity for it. This must express itself in initiatives from their side to discuss particular questions and difficulties with the councils. There would often appear to be a fear of putting

[9] See the Report: *Les structures diocésaines postconciliares* (Secrétariat de liaison entre les Conférences épiscopales d'Europe) (Paris, 1968).

problems forward or talking about them together. If this does not happen, there is a risk that the bishop may come to regard these councils as something of a liability or an attack on himself; the result for the councils is that although they may be allowed to talk about everything, nothing ever comes of it.

IV. THE DIOCESAN SYNODS

The diocesan synods, as envisaged by the *Codex Iuris Canonici,* may best be described as the assembly of bishops with a selected number of priests. In this gathering specific questions are discussed by those present, whilst the decision belongs to the bishop alone, he being the sole signatory to it. Such a synod, which was introduced partly at the instance of Benedict XIV (1740–1758) (in his famous work *De synodo dioecesana*), because consultation with the clergy via the chapter was too deficient, has not taken place in this form in any diocese (as far as I know) since Vatican II. It is not applicable, because lay people have no share in the deliberations; the prescribed representation of priests is inadequate; and the bishop's position, if not in his exclusive right to take decisions, then at any rate in the whole course of the synodal proceedings, has been admitted to be too dominating. Important, then, as a synod may be for the bishop, for the diocese its role is scarcely one of renewal.

If we take a look at the aforementioned councils and a diocesan synod as actually adapted, examining them side by side, it must strike us that they differ in their official aim. The synod's interest is centred on canonically approved decisions; the councils are intended for consultation, discussion and taking counsel and can therefore tolerate a greater freedom both in their composition and further structuring.

Nevertheless, these institutions—councils and synods—tally in this respect: that undergirding both is a desire to set the bishop and the diocesan curias, where the forming and taking of decisions are concerned, more at the centre of the church community. They tend to become institutions in which the diocesan community is, as it were, assembled in concentrated form. They are meant to express a brotherhood, without denying the differences of gifts and responsibilities within it. At the same time a powerful wish emerges that the bishop's mandate should not just be applied more in accordance with his exclusive right as bishop to reach decisions. Here, one may suspect, lies the great challenge to arrive at usages, customs and rules which no longer presuppose the Church to be a society of the *un*equal, but a brotherhood with a common and collective responsibility. But this will be difficult unless there is some measure of agreement about the Church as the people of God and the community of believers.

V. Solving Problems

Should councils which really do function, or regular, well-conducted synods, be able to resolve every problem? Can we expect them to do everything? Of course there are bound to be limiting factors. Conflicts and differences of opinion will arise in the future no less than in the past—perhaps even more so. But less frequently than in the recent past will it be possible for the bishop or his curia simply to dispose of them by a more or less autonomous decision. First and foremost, it would seem desirable for the dioceses, preferably in consultation with the councils and synods, to establish more explicitly, and to publicize, the procedure according to which they propose to settle certain recurrent problems. Often enough a procedure scarcely exists, or it is unknown or is inapplicable. The bishop's decision then seems capricious. It is obvious, too, that the councils or synods, or at any rate the bodies deputed by them, will be involved in the handling of some thorny questions. This can be done in a variety of ways: for instance, they may be officially consulted or enabled to arbitrate. Then there are a considerable number of problems that are common to all the dioceses in a given country, or to large parts of the church community. Often they are of direct and vital relevance to every diocese, yet go beyond the resources and responsibility of the single diocese. However, this may be for a number of different reasons. Certain problems are taken out of the hands of the individual bishop or of the bishops' conferences and reserved to the Holy See in Rome. The sad thing is that nearly everything that decisively affects the personal situation of Catholics falls into that category. I refer on the one hand to the state of life of lay people (marriage, second marriage), priests and religious, and on the other to their position in the church and what they may or may not do. The serious issue here is whether a system of laws which is fixed and which the bishops can neither influence nor infringe does not do harm to a lot of people and kill off new developments—the more so because they invariably start with and relate to particular persons.[10] Again there are problems which a single diocese, at any rate, can hardly cope with, because they have too general a bearing and exceed, for instance, the material and organizational resources of one diocese.

Often that which a diocese, administratively speaking, *may* not and that which it *can*not resolve will in practice be the same thing. Even so, not being *allowed* to settle certain problems at diocesan or national level would seem to get in the way of experimenting and of giving any lead. On this score, one may wonder whether government by bishops, individually or together in a conference, really has a fair chance and is not coming to be a fiction because the opportunities allowed it are so few. There is also a big chance that pastoral councils, priests' senates and diocesan synods will have all too few possibilities, as assemblies of a diocese, for marking out and following up various ways into the future. Stagnation in government must then be the result.

Lastly, we may perhaps make the point that councils and synods in the dioceses can prevent the bishops' conferences or the Synod of Bishops in Rome from becoming isolated bodies.

*   *   *

There is a danger that the diocesan bishop, even despite his good intentions, may remain bogged down in structures and positions which fail adequately to meet the longing to give the Church the form and aspect of a brotherhood. The serious question then is whether this does not give rise to a kind of isolation that makes episcopal administration something remote from the searching, groping local community of believers.

---

[10] Cf. the important conditions desiderated by Vatican II, which have not yet been appraised in their full consequences, in *Christus Dominus*, no. 8.

Translated by Hubert Hoskins

Leonidas Proaño

A Church and Politics in Ecuador

CHAPTERS three and four of the Acts of the Apostles tell of the cure of a man lame from birth and the tumult this action provoked among the people and the authorities. Peter and John preached Christ to the people and spoke boldly of the same Christ before the council: " 'This is the stone that was rejected by you builders'. . . . But seeing the man that had been healed standing beside them, they had nothing to say in opposition. But when they had commanded them to go aside out of the council, they conferred with one another, saying, 'What shall we do with these men? For that a notable sign has been performed through them is manifest to all the inhabitants of Jerusalem, and we cannot deny it. But in order that it may spread no further among the people, let us warn them to speak no more to anyone in this name.' So they called them and charged them not to speak or teach at all in the name of Jesus. But Peter and John answered them, 'Whether it is right in the sight of God to listen to you rather than to God, you must judge; for we cannot but speak of what we have seen and heard.' "[1]

The witness required of us today is the same: to tell what we have seen and heard.

I. A MAN LAME FROM BIRTH

The Latin American country I am reporting on is called Ecuador since it lies on both sides of the Equator. It extends over

[1] Acts 4. 11, 14–20.

270,000 sq. kms. and has rather more than six million inhabitants, who live mainly in the mountains and on the coast.

The country is divided into provinces, each of which has its provincial capital and is in turn subdivided into cantons and further into civil parishes. The capital of the country and also of the province of Pichincha is Quito, which is nearly 9,000 feet above sea level, and has some 500,000 inhabitants. The largest city, and the main port, is Guayaquil; it has nearly 800,000 inhabitants and stands at the mouth of the river Guayas on the Pacific coast.

The country is remarkable for its extraordinary natural beauty and the fertility of its soil: it is the world's major banana exporter and produces an abundance of coffee, rice, cocoa, sugar cane, potatoes, wheat, barley and fruits of all kinds. Large oil deposits have recently been discovered and will soon be exploited.

And yet, despite its magnificent natural advantages, Ecuador contains its man lame from birth: its whole people. Those who study its social structures liken its society to a pyramid, with three per cent of the population living in wealth at the top and the remainder clustering on the sides in conditions varying from poverty to destitution.

II. The Province of Chimborazo

A part of this people lives in the province of Chimborazo, in the geographical centre of the country, covering 6,200 sq. kms. and with some 370,000 inhabitants. Its capital is Riobamba, a city of 50,000 inhabitants, 8,500 feet above sea level, 180 kms. from Quito and 200 from Guayaquil.

Nearly two-thirds of the population are Indians; 73% make their living from agriculture, and by far the greater number of these do not own their own land, but have to work as peons on the big estates, or migrate to the coast for five or six months of the year. The illiteracy rate in the whole country is 32%; in the province of Chimborazo it reaches 54%.

The Diocese of Riobamba. In Ecuador, the institutional Church consists of three archdioceses, ten dioceses, five apostolic vicariates, three prefectures and one *prelatura nullius*. There are thirty prelates: archbishops, bishops, prefects and vicars apostolic; 1,700 priests, secular and religious; 7,800 religious sisters; 180,000 students in Catholic schools, colleges and universities.

The diocese of Riobamba, founded in 1865, is a suffragan of the archdiocese of Quito, with the province of Chimborazo as its territory. It contains sixty secular priests and twenty-three religious; 220 religious sisters belonging to ten congregations; nineteen primary and secondary schools, and one university faculty, teaching agricultural science.

The Local Ecclesial Community. There are three ways of looking at the Church in this post-conciliar period: as immobile, as modernized, or as dynamic.

The immobile view engenders triumphalist, conservative and defensive attitudes, and produces a pastoral approach characterized by conservation, security and alliance—explicit or tacit—with the powers that be.

The modernized view produces superficiality and élitism, and is responsible for a pastoral approach of conservatism mixed with calculated accommodations and adaptations; it "prudently" refrains from confrontation with the "state of sin".

The dynamic view inspires an attitude of faith, or risk-taking, of commitment to the progress of history; its pastoral approach is recognized by its attempt to change the mental and social structures that sin has vitiated; it tries to be faithful, in other words, to the demands of the Gospel.

These three different views of the Church all exist in Ecuador, and can all be found in the diocese of Riobamba. There, within the canonical structure, the local ecclesial community is suffering its birth pangs.

II. Domination and Dependence

1. *The Situation*

The Medellín document on Peace begins with these words: "If development is the new name of peace, the underdevelopment of Latin America, as it exists in varying degrees in different countries, is an unjust situation that promotes tensions which conspire against peace."

In the fields where we work, underdevelopment is a reality

that we see and touch every day. What causes it? Leaving aside
the possibility that, in Latin America, it stems from natural
causes that are almost impossible to overcome, one has to conclude that the appalling state in which our people live is "the
result of an historical development in which dependence and
domination are not fortuitous happenings, but the very texture
and structure of Latin American society".[2]

The relationship between dominators and dominated is shown
in the fact that "few have much (culture, riches, power, pres-
tige), while many have little".[3] There are three outstanding contrasts: few rich—innumerable poor; few with the privilege of
knowledge—masses illiterate and simple; a few able to make
political decisions—the majority deceived or alienated by them.

2. *Critique of the Situation*

The Medellín documents call this state of affairs the "state of
sin". The dominant classes call it the "established order". The
Medellín documents say it is "a positive menace to peace". The
dominant classes "call any attempt to change a system that
favours the continuance of their privileges subversive action",
and "sometimes resort to force in order to crush any attempt at
reaction against them".[4]

It would seem necessary to establish what the word "order"
means. "Peace is, first and foremost, a product of justice. It sup-
poses and requires the establishment of a just order in which
men can realize their human potential, in which their dignity
will be respected, their legitimate aspirations satisfied, their right
to truth recognized, and their personal freedom guaranteed. An
order in which men will be the agents, not the objects, of their
own history."[5]

What is known as the "established order", on the other hand,
is an affront to justice, because it favours a few with an abundance of goods whilst burying the majority in abject poverty; it
is an affront to the order willed by God because, by favouring
selfishness, it perverts the relationship between man and his

---

[2] João Bosco Pinto, *Aportes para la liberación*.
[3] Medellín, *Peace*, 3.
[4] *Ibid.*, 4, 5.
[5] *Ibid.*, 14.

Creator, and his finality with regard to his Creator. By making some men dominators and others dominated, it perverts the relationships between men in community. By making the world the property of a few, it distorts the relationship of dominion over the world that it is the mission of all men to exercise for the perfecting of the world, for the satisfaction of their wants, and for the development of men themselves through the power of their work, their initiatives, their inventiveness and their will to triumph over all obstacles.

3. Complicity of the Church in the Situation

We must recognize, with humble courage, that the Church in Ecuador, as the result of a particular historical process, has been and is involved in the framework of this system, and in basic ways has become an accomplice to the establishment and maintenance of this "state of sin".

With the same humble courage, we must admit that the Church in Riobamba has been enmeshed in the snares of the system and has helped to perpetuate the "state of sin". This has happened through the overwhelming force of the historical process, distorted as it is by selfishness, ambition and pride.

Remembering the three outstanding contrasts noted earlier:

(1) We must confess that the Church in Riobamba owned large tracts of land; that this fact, although thanks to bad management it never made the church rich, gave it the reputation among the poor of being rich; that, along with other local churches, it more than once defended the structures of usurpation and the maintenance of the "established order".

(2) We must confess that the Church in Riobamba has devoted, and still devotes, skilled personnel and economic resources to the education of the children of the privileged few, and that it contributes to the formation in them of a capitalist mentality; that it has not made great enough efforts to educate to freedom the Indians and all those who live under oppression.

(3) We must confess that the Church in Riobamba has not made an effective contribution to changing the condition of its people in such a way that they will be able to participate responsibly in the political life of the country, and that its actions in

this respect have been more likely to favour the continued dominance of one of the ruling classes.

4. Taking a Political Stance

I do not see this as meaning favouring one or other "party".
This was perhaps one of the Church's greatest faults in the past,
when it did so in order to "defend its existing convictions and
positions (on Catholic schools, union of Church and State, marriage, freedom of action, etc.)".[6] I agree rather with those who,
following the Council and the second CELAM conference at
Medellín, see the Church in Latin America as bound to take up
certain positions in the sense that it must continue "proclaiming
the Gospel, but through defence of the rights of the oppressed";
that it must continue intervening in social matters, "not for the
sake of protecting its convictions or pronouncements, but in
order to defend and liberate the oppressed people of Latin
America";[7] that it must "awaken in men and in peoples ... a
lively appreciation of justice"; that it must "protect the rights
of the poor and the oppressed, as the Gospel commands...";
that it must "energetically denounce the abuses and injustices
that stem from the excessive inequality that exists between rich
and poor, between the powerful and the weak...".[8]

5. The Political Stance taken by the Church in Riobamba

The local ecclesial community that is coming to life in Riobamba, in an attempt to remain utterly faithful to the Gospel,
has opted to take up a political stance in the sense expressed
above, and is following a course of action that at once frees it
from its entanglement with the capitalist system and helps to
free the oppressed:

First: It has shed its title of landowner through a series of
covenants designed to bring about agricultural reforms in the
lands that used to belong to it: through this and other steps, it
intends to align itself with the poor.

Second: It is committed to awakening a sense of justice and a
feeling of community among human groups at all levels, through
constant meetings for discussion and planning.

[6] S. Galilea, *La vertiente política de la pastoral.*
[7] *Ibid.*
[8] Medellín, *Peace,* 21, 22, 23.

Third: It has begun to put into practice techniques of educating towards freedom, particularly with groups of young students and peasants.

Fourth: It has denounced abuses and injustices, through the medium of newspapers and other publications started and run by young laymen and priests.

Fifth: Through these means, it is forming a critical awareness among the people, and thus preparing them to participate responsibly in the political life of the country.

*　　　　*　　　　*

This approach and these actions have alarmed some and awakened hopes in others. The violent expulsion of one priest and the imprisonment of another last year, to the accompaniment of many warnings and threats, bear eloquent testimony to the alarm and despondency spreading among the ruling classes as a result of these first attempts of an oppressed people to find its feet, and of one local church to preach freedom in Christ.

Translated by Paul Burns

Antonio Fragoso

The Bishop's Part in Development

AS A citizen of the world, and as a bishop of the Church, I share
in responsibility for human development. As my contribution to
this issue of *Concilium*, I want to set out my thoughts on the
opportunities and possibilities for co-operation in development, on
the basis of my own experience, which seems the most construc-
tive way I can approach the question, and also one within my
own powers. My experience is in the diocese of Crateús. What
we have tried to do here is to find ways to lend a pastoral presence
to the process of development.

I. A SKETCH OF THE HUMAN LANDSCAPE

The diocese of Crateús was founded in 1964 and I am its first
bishop. It extends over 22,000 sq. kms. and in 1970 its population
was around 350,000. It is situated in the heart of the "dry lands",
and is extremely underdeveloped from all points of view:
economic, social, political, cultural and religious. According to
data provided by CEPAL (in *Studies on the Distribution of Income in Latin America*, Santiago, 1967), 50% of the population
of Brazil (45 million) have an annual per capita income of 130
dollars. As the area in which Crateús is situated is one of the
most backward, the annual per capita income is less than this.

Ownership of land is unjustly unequal: in 1968, 12% of the
landowners owned 62% of the land. About half the population
earned its living from the land (rural population 82%), including those who worked in a position of permanent dependency

on land that did not belong to them. The prices of agricultural products are chronically unstable. At the beginning of 1970 a *quarta* (a measure containing 80 litres) of barley was worth $55.00; by the end of the year, the same measure was worth $120.00. In March 1971, when the harvest looked promising, the price dropped to $70.00. Any proper family development is at the mercy of this oscillation, imposed from outside.

The political consciousness of the poor man is virtually non-existent. Electoral campaigns blind him with blandishments, promises, propaganda and pressures. His real freedom to cast his vote as he will is very little. Those in power habitually govern without consulting the organizations that represent the poor, and restrict the right of criticism. A negative and systematic anti-Communism, always on the hunt for "subversives", and the coercion brought to bear on political opposition, make it impossibly difficult for the poor to have any chance of free political expression. Basic education, agricultural training and professional formation are virtually non-existent. The cultural élite, born into families (the local oligarchies) that have grown rich through the common effort, migrate to the great urban centres: this permanent exile of the élite prevents the emergence of any local leadership in development.

II. THE BASIC TROUBLE

It seems to me that these dark aspects of the human landscape hide a basic trouble: *alienation*. Our poor have no confidence in themselves. They do not believe in their creative capacity, or in their historical condition as living images of God the creator. The complex structure of the society in which they live pushes them to one side. It is the rich who decide things, mobilize resources, suppress, and even assist in a paternalistic way. Conscious only of their incapacity and impotence, and stripped of their vocation as subjects for development, the poor accept domination, regional expressions of imperialism and economic dependence. Abject poverty is a disaster whose injurious effects range far and wide: it causes loss of consciousness of human dignity, degrades inner nobility, terrorizes people and makes cowards of them, alienates them from society, increases prostitution, encourages the well-meaning rich to dole out "charity", and is a breeding-ground for political demogogy and ideological agitation.

III. The Church's "Mea Culpa"

I believe the Church to be an accomplice in bringing about this situation. The poor are not to the fore either in its heart or in its pastoral practice. We are in partnership with the oligarchs on whom we are financially dependent. If not in theory, then at least in practice, we accept this bipolarity: he who does not preach capitalism is playing the Communists' game! The fatalism inherent in the alienation of our poor was instilled by our evangelization. We do not know how to turn faith or commitment to the Gospel into a struggle for the integral freedom of man. When we talk of *order*, we fail to distinguish between the historical order that progressively enshrines God's plan, and the established, violent, unjust, oligarchic and discriminatory "order", so-called, under which we live. We defend private property, instead of accepting the consequences of the fact that the benefits of wealth are primarily intended to be used for the good of *all*. We teach respect for authority, and fail to distinguish between its essential meaning of service and its ambiguous historical embodiments. This sort of evangelization is not the soil from which the Church militant, hungering for justice, or fearless prophets of the dignity of the poor and the oppressed, or fighters for a just world of human brotherhood according to God's plan, will spring.

IV. An Active Part in Development

I personally am associated with all the sins and compromises of the Church in my region. Its *"mea culpa"* is mine too. I am also associated with the *prise de conscience* of my fellow bishops of North-Eastern Brazil in their appeals for our involvement in human development. In my pastoral letter of greeting to the poor of Crateús (9 August 1964), I said: "God sent me to Crateús to announce to all, rich and poor, great and small, the good news of God's love. To welcome all who freely want to come into the family of the Church. And, as a humble servant, to lead all who wish to their final destiny, the kingdom of God, happy and per-fect, in heaven. This is my essential task. But it is also the bishop's task to proclaim the conditions for the construction of a just, human and brotherly world that can be the continuation of the loving creation of God. And to remind Christians, in the con-sciousness of their responsibility, to engage themselves, like all men of good will, in social institutions, so as to make the city of men worthy of being inhabited by the sons of God. And to educate Christians so that together they will try to make the values of the Gospel live in this earthly city."

Such were the words of the new bishop just entered into his diocese. Today, they look poetic and pretty enough, but coming down to earth through the realism imposed by the march of events, I would stress even more strongly that the bishop must be involved in the development of his diocese, of his region, and of the world.

V. Gradual Discoveries

The ups and downs of joint pastoral effort, with the faithful and the clergy, convince me more and more that:

—The bishop is not the leader in implanting civilization in his area.

—His mission is not that of a technician in human develop-ment.

—All human development, as an historical expression of God's plan, concerns him vitally.

—As a man of faith, by calling, and a teacher of faith, he should be accessible to, and welcome, any honest attempt to im-plant development, and all ideologies and doctrinary assertions, in an adult, brotherly and truthful dialogue.

—His faith, immanent in the historical process that develop-ment constitutes, should not exhaust itself in it, but illumine it with a global vision of man and his destiny, with a hope that is at once certainty and utopia.

—His prophetic mission compels him to denounce everything that is anti-human in all Development Plans and in all ideologies.

—His prophetic mission, universal as that of Christ, while making him welcome all men whatever their ideology, should prevent him from aligning himself with particular political groups that would cut him off from other men.

VI. THE STEPS TAKEN IN CRATEÚS

Since the bishop is not a remote figure presiding in solitary eminence over his "flock of sheep", but a brother who emerges from among the Christian poor so as to set them on their historical course, inspiring them in the name of God, and being inspired in his turn by the same poor, it would seem that his pastoral effort must be all-embracing, neither clerical nor lay. So we started sessions for the clergy and lay delegates from the parishes, lasting on average twenty days, for reflection on the pastoral situation and the pastoral approach required. This enabled everyone to form a joint view of the problem, without forcing the pace of discovery for anyone, and without hindering the appearance of tensions, fears, uncertainties and disagreements. The constant preoccupation is always to refer everything to the present reality, to lead towards a critical analysis of pastoral initiatives in the light of the life that the poor really live, and to debate the impact of structures and ideologies on the behaviour and faith of the poor.

We were convinced that the basic trouble for the poor was their alienation. To try to overcome this, gradually and within the limitations of our abilities, we began to encourage the development of communities in the villages and city districts. The members of the communities began by meeting to discuss their problems, needs and possibilities. They then reflect on the meaning of what they have found out, together. In response to this, they then try to *act*, either in small communitarian ways themselves, or by seeking wider support. Each community project opens their eyes and makes them *see* and *feel* that they are capable of development, that they are the *subject* of human growth in the community, and they then begin gradually to free themselves from the local oligarchical pattern of leadership which so exploited them.

They then reflect on communitarian action, together with the diocesan advisers, and find it to be insufficient: inter-communitarian action becomes necessary. Then the discovery of the structures that condition them leads them to professional action through the Unions or the Co-operative. The most clear-sighted among them discover that the laws of the country, and the dominance of economic over political power, force them to political action in an enlightened attempt to reduce the power of the minority groups and to secure the free participation of the poor in the process of human development. This is where different ideologies come into conflict with each other, when radical groups of the extreme Right and Left challenge the conscience of the bishop, the clergy and the faithful of the diocese. How does one integrate growth in faith, presence in development, and an honest dialogue with all ideological groups? The seductive influence exercised by radical groups of the extreme Left on the best of our young people is an impressive fact. The parochial and diocesan structures of the Church do not offer the same perspectives or mystique of the struggle for justice, vitally committed to Christ and his Church and at the same time to the freedom of man within the process of history.

*　　　*　　　*

Such is my "testament", the story of a timid pastoral attempt. It calls for the publication of other "testaments" from bishops of other dioceses—richer, poorer, or more blessed than mine. Might not *Concilium* become the vehicle for such publications, and so the forum for a permanent dialogue between the theologian and the pastor, in the context of the pastoral reality of today?

Translated by Paul Burns

Paul Moore, Jr.

The Witness of the Bishop in the Local Church

IT WAS the summer of 1964 in McComb, Mississippi. The bishop
celebrated on an ironing board, behind him the reredos was the
side of a bombed-out Civil Rights headquarters, laid bare by the
Ku Klux Klan a few days before; the gospel, by complete coinci-
dence, was Luke 19. 41. "And when he was come near, he beheld
the city and wept over it, saying, If thou hadst known even
thou at least in this thy day, the things that belong unto thy
peace! But now they are hid from thine eyes." The Holy Sacrifice included the lives of workers, recently slain and the fear and
persecution of the Black people of Mississippi.

It was the summer of 1970 in Saigon, South Vietnam. The
congregation consisted of Vietnamese students, Catholic priests,
Buddhist monks, and mothers who had lost their sons through
arrest or in the war. The leaders of the gathering were a young
man fresh out of the Tiger Cages, the student president deaf in
one ear as a result of police torture, part of the "liturgy" the
bringing forward, in a ghastly offertory procession (so it seemed),
of a miniature coffin swinging on a pole suspended on the
shoulders of two wrinkled old mothers. They presented the
coffin to the American bishop with these words: "The gift of
the Vietnamese people to the American people, our dead." After
this solemn moment, the peace procession formed and we issued
forth on the street, only to be dispersed with tear gas a few
moments later.

A bishop should build the structure and spirit of his diocese
and lead as he can in ecumenical groupings so that the daily life

of his clergy and people provide social service and social action in a sustained orderly fashion. But also, from time to time, he should step out into more dramatic and controversial action. For his office still carries a heavy symbolism in the eyes of the world as well as the eyes of the Church. And there are times for this apostolic gift to be put on the line. If the Church is to witness to the love of Christ, if the Church is to be criticized for standing on the side of justice, certainly the bishop, the chief pastor, should lead in this witness. And it is strange how often the culmination of these actions takes on a liturgical cast.

One becomes involved in such actions more by providence than by calculation, it seems. You may remember the atmosphere in the United States in the summer of 1964. The Civil Rights movement was gathering momentum and many churchmen from the North were going South to stand beside their brothers. Although some of the motivation for this was ambiguous and romantic, none the less it seemed clearly a movement inspired by the Holy Spirit. I was weighing, prudentially, the decision to go South, when I happened to hear a sermon on the text: "Launch out into the deep" (Luke 5. 3). This decided me to go to Mississippi. The peace mission to Saigon came about through the call of a friend. Participation in a controversial boycott in Washington grew out of a long and complicated series of events.

By mentioning the liturgical quality of some of my own experiences, and the way in which I became involved in such events, I wish to put forward the notion that a bishop's taking sides on social issues, whether local, national, or international, is not something which ordinarily occurs because of set principles worked out by commissions and general councils, but rather out of the mix of events, out of previous experiences, out of the kind of friends you are drawn to, out of a chance passage of Scripture coming to you at the right moment, out of the life-style that informs your work. And so it is that the more you allow yourself to be buried in the administration and pastoral work of the institution, important though it be, the less likely you are to witness, the less likely you will be invited to take a stand. I find it necessary, every year or two, to get out on the streets, as it were, to regain my perspective, to hear and see the sights and sounds of suffering humanity more intensely than usual. I also try to keep especially close communication with some of the younger clergy who are in social movements and close to the logic of the militant, to redress the bias of those more prominent churchmen whom a bishop usually sees.

Many legitimate pressures pull a bishop back from the courage of witness. People criticize us for being too concerned with money, but do they realize that less money means less resources with which to serve the poor, less money means clergy and their families without income? The pressures are tortuous because you are sacrificing others, not yourself, for the cause. I am conscious, too, of the kind of sacrifice a parish priest is called upon to make when his bishop witnesses. Not only does he lose people and money but often that dearly-won unity he has worked so long to attain.

However, there is a positive side for the parish as well. A bishop's witness is a glorious opportunity for education. In fact, the more controversial the action the more emotionally involved people become, and therefore, the more open they are to hearing the rationale behind the action as well as the issues spoken to. A wise pastor can use such an occasion more happily than if he himself is witnessing and therefore on the defensive. A bishop's stand frees up the clergy and laity to be more forceful in their own work, for he enables and legitimizes their action.

It might be useful to discuss some of the framework within which one makes a witness. This is a time of collegiality. Unilateral decisions by the hierarchy are frowned on. Decentralization and participatory democracy are the cry. In this context I have often been accused of doing or saying something without consulting the clergy or without notifying them ahead of time. This is a legitimate point. When a bishop speaks, even as an individual, he is speaking to some extent, in the minds of some people, for the Church; therefore the Church has some right to participate in the decisions he makes. On the other hand, because of the very nature of social action, because so often it must be taken quickly in order to have an effect, consultation is frequently impossible. Better, perhaps, than formal consultation issue by issue, is an ongoing open conversation with clergy and lay leaders about the issues in society and about the style of the Church's involvement in them. In this way they will come to know the mind of the bishop and be able to interpret him to the people, and he will come to know their mind and the degree to which he would upset them by a certain method of witness.

In this ecumenical age, witness is far stronger when spoken by the whole Christian, or better yet, by the whole religious community. And yet again it is often impossible to rally different religious leaders around in time to respond to an issue, if you do not have an ongoing ecumenical structure. Here again, a bishop has great leadership strength by virtue of his office, even amongst Protestants and Jews, I think the greatest failing of bishops around the world, until recently at least, was their failure to take seriously their responsibility for Christian unity of witness and action.

Another aspect of the problem, brought up most frequently by older churchmen, has to do with the dignity of the bishop. I have often heard people say, "Well, it is all right for other people to march on the streets, but a bishop shouldn't." The dramatic quality of a bishop's involvement, its very news-worthi-ness, is a reason to take to the streets from time to time. And certainly, in our day, words have lost some of their effectiveness. Thus prophetic action is more frequently called for. Now that marches are losing their novelty, we may have to go in some other direction.

I imagine it is quite clear by now that I feel a bishop should forcefully witness in his local community as well as in wider fields. The age we live in lends itself to this style because the institution with which we have been preoccupied is beginning to crumble despite our prudence and diligent administration. The energy and power which can be gained by witness feeds our lives and enables us to be more creative in envisioning the shape of the Church to come, and by its very nature draws us ever closer, in a natural, unself-conscious way, to our brothers of other persuasions. For, after all, our Lord's major concern in his lifetime was for the Kingdom more than for his Church. By witnessing on local issues we learn who our brothers are in the Kingdom.

To conclude, the bishop as chief pastor represents the Church more than any other person. The image he projects affects the image of the Church and enhances or denigrates the image of Christ. If the function of the Church can be described as showing forth Christ, then the bishop's witness is absolutely essential.

He must be clear and sure of his facts. The issue must be weighty enough to warrant his attention. If possible he should establish criteria for his own guidance and discuss them with his councils of advice. Although it is helpful to seek counsel in specific actions, in the last analysis the decision must be his own, made with prudence and wisdom but, more importantly, with courage and passion.

Ultimately the rationale for his involvement has to do with his role as celebrant of the Eucharist. If he lifts up the suffering of humanity on the altar he cannot fail to witness for his suffering people, God's people, in the struggle for justice. As celebrant of the Eucharistic Kingdom, he supports and urges forward the signs of that Kingdom in earth, for he is an apostle sent to all men, not just a pastor of his own.

He will find that Kingdom as he gets out of the Church and meets Christ in the poor as he meets Christ on the altar.

Bibliography

Reckitt, Maurice Benington, *Maurice to Temple; a century of the social movement in the Church of England* (London, 1947). A discussion of the Church and social problems, within the Church of England.

Temple, William, *Christianity and the Social Order* (London and New York, 1942). Another classic in the experience of the Episcopacy as it sought to understand its function within the social order.

Westcott, Brooke Foss, *Social Aspects of Christianity* (London, 1900). A discussion of some aspects of the elements of social life, with insight into the organization of social life.

Huddleston, Trevor, *Naught for your Comfort* (London, 1956). The Bishop of Masai, South Africa, describes his battle for housing and native resources in Johannesburg.

Rahner, Karl, *Bishops, their Status and Function* (London, 1965).

Stringfellow, William, *Free in Obedience* (New York, 1964).

Willie, Charles V., *Church Action in the World* (New York, 1965). A young Black sociologist takes a more radical look at the "Church Active".

PART II
BULLETIN

Frans Haarsma

Consensus in the Church: Is an Empirical Inquiry Possible?

THE editors of *Concilium* ask for a discussion of "published matter dealing with the value of inquiries designed to establish whether there is a consensus in the Church or in a part of the Church". Documents which handle this question—as it is put here—and attempt to provide a direct and explicit answer are not known to me; and so I cannot in the strict sense satisfy the terms of the editors' request. What I can do, however, is to set out a few reflections that may perhaps have a bearing on any future study of this problem. They have to do with the theological concept of "consensus", the potentialities and limits of social research that make use of such inquiries, and the presuppositions underlying the question itself. The obvious thing would be to start with this last item; but I have preferred to leave it to the end, because if they are to be fairly evaluated, such critical comments as I have to make must be seen in the light of the earlier sections.

I. CONSENSUS

Theological literature distinguishes between the *sensus fidei* (the sense of faith) and *consensus fidelium* (the agreement of the faithful), sometimes more closely defined as *universalis* or *unanimis*.[1] The sense (*sensus*) of faith has been defined as one

---

[1] M. Seckler, "Glaubenssin", in *L.Th.K.* IV (²1960), pp. 945–8; *Mysterium Salutis* III (Hilversum/Antwerp, 1967), pp. 78–89; M. Dominikus Koster, "Der Glaubenssinn der Hirten und Gläubigen", in *Id., Volk Gottes im Werden. Gesammelte Studien* (Mainz, 1971), pp. 131–50.

which, arising as it does out of faith, gives reason for everything that has relevance to that faith. It is a spontaneous, non-discursive mode of knowing, analogous to the "clinical eye" of the medical practitioner. The consensus of the faithful is a result of the sense of faith and presupposes it. It has been more precisely defined as a unanimous expression of belief by the totality of the faithful, arising out of the sense. The consensus would be something statistically confirmable, whereas the sense must be grounded in theology. Furthermore, the sense is said to be infallible, but also to be subject to checking, and critical interpretation, on the part of the teaching authority. This last is necessary because the sense as such is not directly accessible, but only via objectivizing factors of confession, witness, formal worship and active Christian commitment. Yet these objectivizing factors are by no means an adequate and unambiguous expression of the sense of faith. The complicated relations between the authentic teaching office, the infallible sense and the consensus of the faithful as a form of expression are to be found in the much quoted passage from the chapter on the People of God in the Vatican II Constitution on the Church: "The body of the faithful as a whole, anointed as they are by the Holy One (cf. 1 Jn. 2. 20, 27), cannot err in matters of belief. Thanks to a supernatural sense of the faith which characterizes the People as a whole, it manifests this unerring quality when, 'from the bishops down to the last member of the laity', it shows universal agreement in matters of faith and morals. For, by this sense of faith which is aroused and sustained by the Spirit of truth, God's people accepts not the word of men but the very Word of God (cf. 1. Th. 2. 13). It clings without fail to the faith once delivered to the saints (cf. Jude 3), penetrates it more deeply by accurate insights, and applies it more thoroughly to life" (*Lumen Gentium*, no. 12).

This passage is coming to be regarded as one of the most important achievements of Vatican II. In a climate of democratizing and re-evaluating the place of the layman it was bound to go down well; yet it bristles with snares and pitfalls which a critical theology cannot just take in its stride. Thus one might raise the question whether it makes sense to speak of an *infallible sense of faith*, when at the same time one has to concede that the form in which that sense is expressed may well be quite inadequate and ambiguous, in other words, is not infallible. Could not this arguably be a relic of dualism, which introduces a separation where what is really in place is simply a distinction between two aspects? Can one and the same human act of faith be fallible in one aspect and infallible in another? Or have we to set out the one act of faith in different stages and say of a first, invisible, interior stage that it is infallible, whilst denying this of a later stage of expression? But then what is this infallibility, which eludes every form of testing? Now it may be objected that the *sensus* is not an act but an organ, a faculty that makes infallible believing possible. As I see it, this offers no solution. The difficulty is still what is the meaning of calling an organ infallible when the acts of faith that arise from it do not turn out to be infallible. But enough of this: *à propos* of our subject, we must get back to the consensus of the faithful.

The consensus of the faithful is an important theological notion, because it not only functions as a bit of natural ground for theology but is used by the magisterium as one of the criteria for defining the authentic faith of the Church. I take for granted here some knowledge of the theological grounding; where I would like to focus attention is on the difficulties one is up against as soon as one sets out to define this concept more precisely. The first is: who are meant by the *faithful* or by the *Church*, if it is a question of the consensus of the faithful or of a consensus in the Church? In this context the question of whether we have to include bishops, clergy and theologians here is of secondary importance. Of course they are part of it—but *not* in as much as they have a mission and responsibility distinct from those of the rest of the faithful. They belong as members of the People of God, as Augustine says: "For I am a bishop for you; but with you I am a Christian" (*Lumen Gentium*, no. 32). The problem arises as soon as we ask: where is the people of Christ as a theologically qualified entity to be found?[2] By way of a reply we read: "Essentially, what 'Christian people' means in this context is the community of those who through baptism and confirmation have come to partake in the offices of Christ ... in so far as they reveal themselves to be such and in one form

[2] M. Löhrer, in *Mysterium Salutis, loc. cit.*; see note 1 above.

or another confess and affirm their faith."[3] And then is added—rightly enough: "This sort of manifestation can, of course, include a large range of differences in density and breadth of variation (part of the reason being that the 'Christian people' is not an easy-to-grasp theological locus)." Thus the difficulty returns, large as life, to confront us.

One thing, certainly, is clear: after Vatican II, Christians of other confessions cannot be excluded. It is *not* clear whether and how the qualitative differences between believers are to be evaluated. This is the more true because in teaching about the *sensus fidei* it is rightly argued that the latter is indeed given to each believer along with the charisma of faith (at baptism, perhaps? or only when one can say that faith is present and real, as a believing response to the Gospel when it is heard?), but that its intensity is bound up with the existential realization of faith; so that it could possibly shrivel up and die away altogether. In order, therefore, to ascertain a consensus in the Church (naturally, on matters of faith and morals and on the resultant line of pastoral action, internal as well as external) are we then to take account only of true, authentic believers? But then the question arises as to who does the selecting, and according to what criteria. If we allocate the task to the ecclesiastical authorities and they determine the criteria, the only possible outcome of that will be a vicious circle: we are settling in advance just what we want to find out, and the result will (infallibly) conform to it. The infallibility of the faithful, as the criterion and locus of belief, then becomes a dead letter. If we make all baptized persons or even all practising Christians party to this, then a certain consensus might be established, but without any guarantee that it will be in accord with gospel truth, certainly when it comes to really current problems of Christian living, such as concrete responsibility for world peace, for the rights of minorities or of co-operation for development. One has only to think of how the President of Pax Christi International, Cardinal Alfrink, has reproached Catholics for doing far too little for peace, or of the poor response among broad sections of the Catholics in wealthy countries to the Encyclical *Populorum Progressio*. Thus there is

[3] M. Löhrer, *loc. cit.*, p. 80.

no assurance at all in this case that the consensus is the locus of infallibly true *belief*.

This brings us to a second problem that presents itself as soon as we take a closer look at consensus as a theological concept: *consensus regarding what?* For what "matters of Christian doctrine" (Newman) can the consensus of the faithful be used as an infallible criterion? Theologians like Melchior Cano and Scheeben have very clear reservations on this point: those questions, of course, which are not beyond anyone's understanding, and even then more for the essential, basic thing than for the explanation and working out of detail—but not matters for which a higher standard of education and greater experience are necessary, and which are therefore reserved for the judgment of experts in the Church. What these may be, in a concrete sense, or what criterion one should lay down for them remains obscure. In fact the consensus of the faithful has operated in recent times in respect of the promulgation of two dogmas—the Immaculate Conception and the Assumption of Mary—and of hardly anything else. The theologians who instance this, however, go on to say that the consensus of the faithful "is not exactly a factor to which an uncritical appeal can be made for new declarations of dogma. It is precisely in cases of this sort that critical interpretation, especially the continual resumption of contact with Scripture as the primary, unconditioned norm, cannot be dispensed with."[4] Really and truly, therefore, the consensus operates, not as an infallible criterion for establishing the truth of doctrine, but as confirmation of what has already been officially enunciated. Does this perhaps give it more the character of a *negative* criterion? If the body of believers were to oppose the defining of a dogma which the Pope had proposed, that would be a relevant factor in the process of forming a judgment. Yet even in this negative sense it is not a decisive factor, as is evident from the fact that the variety of practice and ideas regarding contraception among the greater part, or at any rate a very important part, of Catholics did not deter Paul VI from promulgating the encyclical *Humanae Vitae*.

The next difficulty arises when one asks how the putative consensus comes about, from what factor it *derives* as an infallible assent of faith. One factor has been mentioned already: the sense

[4] M. Löhrer, *loc. cit.*, p. 88.

of faith. Yet this is a personal, individual gift, and part and parcel of the grace of faith. There can be no question of an infallible concurrence of belief or consensus, unless it receives general and virtually unanimous expression; which is why we speak, albeit in a figurative sense, of a sense of faith of the whole Church, without elaborating on it further than that. It is clear from all this that the sense of faith cannot provide a satisfactory explanation for the emergence of an infallible consensus in the Church: actually, the moment it is objectivized, the guarantee of infallibility is no longer there. So we are again directed to the function of the teaching office in the Church. The Holy Spirit, we are told, keeps the faith at all times inviolate in the community of the Church as a whole. Not simply by a direct operation upon the individual believer but also through the mediatory function of the visible magisterium. The consensus of the faithful implies a "passive" infallibility of the listening Church—not, therefore, an organ of independent criticism standing over against the magisterium. It is rather that the listening Church possesses its infallibility precisely in conjoining with the authentic teaching authority.[5] Obviously, it is impossible by this means to make the general agreement of the faithful, in the sense of an infallible criterion for belief, a manageable notion with which the theologian can work. It results in more confusion than clarification.

The scope of this article does not permit us to open up the complete background to the concept of a consensus of the faithful. This has been done up to a point in recent studies of *infallibility*, a notion belonging "to the as yet unmastered past of Vatican I" and calling for "a new, more profound interpretation".[6] If this applies to the infallibility of the teaching office, it should be clear from the above analysis that it is no less true—perhaps even more so—of the infallibility of the consensus of the faithful.

But it is not only that the infallibility of the consensus needs

---

[5] H. Bacht, "Consensus", in *L.Th.K.* III (²1959), chs. 43–46.

[6] W. Kasper, in *Publik* of 12.12.1969, cited by H. Küng, *Unfehlbar? Eine Anfrage* (Zürich, Einsiedeln and Cologne, ²1970), pp. 162-3; see also G. Thils, *L'Infaillibilité pontificale. Source-Conditions-Limites* (Gembloux, 1969); *Infallibility in the Church. An Anglican-Catholic Dialogue* (London, 1968); E. Castelli (ed.), *L'Infaillibilité. Son aspect philosophique et théologique* (Paris, 1970).

a new and deeper interpretation; the notion of a *consensus unanimis et universalis* is evidently not so operational as its use in theological treatises would suggest. Neither subject nor object is accurately definable without the officially enunciated doctrine being directly involved. The biggest difficulty, however, arises from this: that the consensus of the faithful is indeed presented as being brought about by the Holy Spirit, but still as a given *fact*, whereas in reality it might well be a *task*—always to be desiderated, of course, yet never completely attained. This is something that may well go along with the tendency in Catholic ecclesiology to anticipate the eschatological fulfilment. One might also put it like this: "A theological proposition is often a judgment as to value *and* a judgment as to fact. It aims to describe a particular reality in its essence, but this essence forms at the same time a positive or negative norm for conduct."[7] The fact that in theology people are not always conscious of this, or at any rate do not state clearly whether they have this or that in view, makes co-operation between theology and sociology extremely difficult.

This brings us to a point that constitutes a natural passage to the second part of this article on the value of inquiries. In order to obviate misunderstanding, however, I would like to state quite explicitly that criticism of the Church's theological doctrine about the consensus of the faithful does not mean that it is held to be of no value whatever. On the contrary, I am convinced that it enshrines a true and very valuable intuition. It is the intuition that *dialogue and communication* are the necessary ways by which the Holy Spirit keeps the Church in the faith and gives it a deeper understanding of the truth thereof.[8]

II. The Value of Inquiries

Although, so far as I know, there are no studies that explicitly tackle the question of the value of inquiries aimed at determining

[7] J. Dhooghe, "Quelques problèmes posés par le dialogue entre Sociologie et Théologie pastorale", in *Social Compass* 17 (1970), pp. 215-29, quot. p. 220.

[8] This has been very nicely elaborated, among other things in its consequences for the function of the magisterium, by W. Kasper, "Zum Problem der Rechtgläubigkeit in der Kirche von Morgen", in F. Haarsma, W. Kasper, W. Kaufmann, *Kirchliche Lehre—Skepsis der Gläubigen* (Freiburg, 1970), pp. 37-96.

whether there is a consensus in (a part of) the Church, in the commentaries and subsequent reflections prompted by various sociological investigations within the area of Church and religion there has been some fairly thorough discussion of these kind of researches, their limits and potentialities, with theology and the principles of pastoral activity in view. Very disparate conclusions have been drawn. More often than not, theologians and in particular the men responsible for ecclesiastical policy adopt a deprecatory tone. They argue that a statistical investigation like *God in Nederland* says nothing about what people really believe, gives a totally false picture of the real situation, that a questionnaire narrowly structured with a view to statistical breakdown is not a sufficiently refined instrument for measuring the variegated forms in which a sense of religion and of the Church can be expressed.[9] The investigators reply—rightly, I believe—that those who condemn the method of inquiry are for the most part the very people who are disappointed or feel themselves threatened by the results. The factors responsible for this are chiefly a lack of familiarity with the method, the conviction that a demonstrated statistical regularity is incompatible with human freedom, and above all the sense that one is being somehow indicted by the results.

They do of course admit—and this would apply just as much to an inquiry such as *Was glauben die Deutschen?* (What do Germans believe?)[10]—that one does not get answers "in depth" through an investigation of this sort. In other words, an inquiry is not an appropriate means for finding out from those questioned what is the nature of faith, as defined in theology and envisaged as the aim of preaching and pastoral work, in all its dimensions. This applies specifically to the quality, personal appropriation, and existential choice, which are essential dimensions of Christian faith. Should we want to get at these dimensions, we would have to mount an investigation into the "faith posture" by means of what are known as "non-directive" interviews, combined if necessary with the method of participative observation. Kaufmann rightly points out that pastoral

[9] *God in Nederland* (Amsterdam, 1967), pp. 18 ff.
[10] W. Harenberg (ed.), *Was glauben die Deutschen? Die Emnid-Umfrage. Ergebnisse. Kommentare* (Munich, 1968).

conversation really offers a much broader prospect here. The situation is then that of a "from faith to faith" dialogue, in which faith can emerge as an intersubjective assurance.[11] Over against this is the fact that with such pastoral dialogue one has overstepped the bounds of socio-scientific research. Of course, a series of pastoral conversations, accurately recorded, do lend themselves to a theological-cum-psychological analysis in the form of a "case study".[12]

The question remains: what then is the value of investigations such as *God in Nederland, Was glauben die Deutschen?* and above all the inquiry, already carried out (but not as yet interpreted) among Catholics in Germany regarding the joint Synod of the dioceses in the Federal Republic? Perhaps this is best put in the words of H. D. Bastian: they acquaint us with *homo religiosus statisticus*.[13] They reveal the extent to which certain religious ideas are firmly rooted in the public consciousness of a particular nation, a part of the Church or a group of the faithful —for instance, priests.[14] They reveal, too, how these ideas go along with an attitude to the Church as a social system, to its leaders, officials, laws and religious practices, how they tie up with its relation to other Churches, with the store it sets by values and ideals that exist outside the orbit of the Church. The importance of this for theology and church government and policy is rather like that of the automatic pilot for modern aviation. Just as the pilot of a jet-propelled aircraft cannot rely on feeling to help him determine height and speed, theology and the Church,

[11] W. Kaufmann, "Zur Rezeption soziologischer Einsichten in die Theologie", in *Kirchliche Lehre—Skepsis der Gläubigen*, pp. 97–127; see also, *Id.*, "Fragen der Soziologie an die christliche Theologie", in H. Vorgrimmler, R. van der Gucht, *Bilanz der Theologie im 20. Jahrhundert*, *B.I.* (Freiburg, 1969), pp. 246–68.

[12] The department of pastoral theology at Nijmegen has carried out such a study under the direction of Dr. W. Berger and Dr. W. Zandbelt; a group of students have analysed nine series of pastoral discussions on *Change and hope* (p.m.).

[13] H. D. Bastian, "Theologie als Marktforschung", in *Was glauben die Deutschen?* pp. 152–71.

[14] For instance, *Ambtscelibaat in een veranderende kerk. Resultaten van een onderzoek onder alle priesters, diakens en subdiakens in Nederland* (Clerical celibacy in a changing Church. Results of an inquiry among all priests, deacons and subdeacons in The Netherlands), pub. by the Pastoral Institute of the Dutch Province (Rotterdam, 1969).

when it comes to their diagnosis and their line of conduct, cannot rely on vague guesses and impressions[15] in the highly organized and extremely complex society we live in. This kind of sociological research into religion gives the theologian an insight into how society and culture condition the religious consciousness of the individual, so that some influence, either positive or corrective, may be brought to bear.

It follows from all this that sociological research in the religious field cannot yield any direct answer to theological questions—including thus the theological question of what we are to understand by a consensus of the faithful. Such research does, however, give the theologian something to think about.[16] In this connection it is as well to remember that the sociologists are most keen to pursue discriminative questions, as they call them, questions which "get somewhere"; which means that they are set on tracking down opposed, or at any rate deviant, tendencies which will enable them to construct their typologies and thereby illustrate the connections and correlations between a number of options and attitudes. Questions to which all the respondents give the same reply are of little or no interest to them. This is one more indication that for establishing a consensus—even in the faith, to the extent that this is alive in the public consciousness—one has little to hope for from this kind of investigations. Rather, what they serve to reveal is a *dissensus*, an expression of disagreement regarding certain until now generally accepted ideas and officially upheld formulations in the sphere of faith and morals.

III. The Demand for the Consensus

Questions which as part of an inquiry invoke an almost 100% unanimous reply are not questions of interest. The point at issue is then self-evident, is not problematical in any way, and is divorced from what is actually going on. Therefore the question of whether it is possible to establish a universal and unanimous

---

[15] H. D. Bastian, *op. cit.*, p. 153.
[16] *Ambtcelibaat in een veranderende kerk*, p. 199; cf. also E. Schillebeeckx, "Kerk en godsdienstsociologie", in *De Zending van de Kerk* (Bilthoven, 1968), pp. 287–309: previously published in *Tijdschrift voor Theologie* 2 (1962), pp. 55–76, and in *Social Compass* 10 (1963), pp. 257–84.

consensus loses a great deal of its value. The notion of consensus as employed in current theology belongs more to a static conception of the Church than to a dynamic one, a uniform rather than a pluriform conception, an authoritarian-cum-hierarchical conception rather than a charismatic one. The concept is correlative with that of infallibility, and creates the same misunderstandings. Not only in sociology but in theology the concept with which we shall have to work is that of *dissensus*. For "in and through the Church there is continuously taking place the eschatological conflict with the powers of falsehood, error and the lie; according to the firmness of our faith truth will again and again prevail and never finally go under. Hence, in the conflict centred upon a right knowledge of the truth, the Church, by reason of its faith, can be a sign of hope for human society. It must testify by its own example that it is never senseless but in fact a continuing necessity to search, and to go on in the assurance that the truth will persist."[17] Sociological inquiry is an indispensable aid to finding out just where the tight corners in this struggle are to be found.

[17] W. Kasper, *art. cit.*; see note 6 above.

Translated by Hubert Hoskins

Franz Josef Kötter

The Value of German-language Catechisms in obtaining a Consensus of Faith

I. The Investigation in a Theological Context

IN any attempt to obtain a consensus of faith in the German-speaking parts of Europe, it is undoubtedly valuable to study the Catholic catechisms produced in those areas, because both the origin and the effects of those catechisms have always been associated with a theological problem intimately linked with the whole question of "consensus of faith". This problem was raised in the Constitutions on Divine Revelation and the Church (especially arts. 12 and 35) of Vatican II and can be very baldly summarized as "teaching office of the Church *v.* faith of the Christian community".

God's revelation, which might be described as a salvific community between God and men, is given to the Church as a whole. This new people of God is not, of course, unorganized, but structured, and features office and community in their variously non-transferable, specific functions, especially in so far as the reception, transmission and the interpretation of revelation are concerned. The community as a whole, however, is not simply passive in comparison with the Church's office in the matter of revelation. The two depend on and flow into one another—it is in this way that the Church remains faithful to God and allows his revelation to unfold fully.[1] This mutual dependence and merging together in German catechisms can be seen from two

---

[1] See B. van Leeuwen, "Die allgemeine Teilnahme am Prophetenamt Christi", in G. Baraúna, *De Ecclesia*, Vol. I (Freiburg, 1966), pp. 393-419.

points of view—their origin and development, and their effects. I think it is preferable to examine the phenomenon of catechisms from these two standpoints in order to see how they testify to faith as existing in the Church and how they have influenced that faith.

II. The Origin and Aim of Catechisms

As statements about faith and means of instruction, catechisms have played an important part for more than four hundred years in the German-speaking world. The term "catechism" extended its meaning from the instruction of catechumens in the early Church to that of religious education generally in the Middle Ages,[2] with the result that a new literary *genre* emerged at the Reformation, when "catechism" became the technical term for a book used in religious education. This development originated with Luther's catechisms of 1529, which were followed by a far greater number of Catholic catechisms than is generally imagined, long before the appearance of Peter Canisius' works and the *Catechismus Romanus*.[3]

Two types can be distinguished—those for teaching and those for learning—but, with a few exceptions, two features are common to both. In the first place, they aim to make Catholic doctrine kerygmatically fruitful in pastoral work and to serve the proclamation of faith. It should be obvious, of course, that the modern distinction between systematic, speculative theology and kerygmatic theology does not apply strictly to these earlier works, but their aim was undoubtedly to serve what Karl Rahner has called the characteristic of genuine kerygmatic theology, namely, "the *kerygma* of the Church, the fruitful and efficacious proclamation of the saving message of Christ".[4] In the second place, they aim to set out the whole teaching of Catholic faith systematically. This is usually done within the framework of the four

[2] See J. Hofinger, "Katechismus", in *LThK*, Vol. 6 (Freiburg, [6]1961), p. 45.

[3] See F. J. Kötter, *Die Eucharistielehre in den katholischen Katechismen des 16. Jahrhunderts bis zum Erscheinen des Catechismus Romanus (1566)* (Münster, 1969), pp. 24–111.

[4] See K. Rahner, "Kerygmatische Theologie", *LThK*, Vol. 6 (Freiburg, [2]1961), p. 126.

catechetical elements evolved in Catholic catechesis in the course of history—the Apostles' Creed, the Our Father, the Ten Commandments and the Sacraments.[5] By and large, this aim has been preserved throughout the centuries with very pronounced changes in emphasis, mainly because of the needs of apologetics and controversy. Attempts were made during the Enlightenment to stress a rational religion and the pre-eminence of ethics and, during the Romantic period, to emphasize the Bible and salvation history. From the middle of the nineteenth century until the middle of the twentieth, neo-Scholasticism prevailed; this was replaced round about 1955 by a catechism oriented towards salvation history (*Der katholische Katechismus der Bistümer Deutschlands*). This catechism, which was also very complete and systematic, still exerts considerable influence in Germany, but a surprisingly short time after its publication the purpose and above all the use of such a catechism in schools were radically questioned.

One further factor should be borne in mind. Until the middle of the eighteenth century, catechisms were addressed to all believers. Afterwards, however, with the "transition to an obligatory and—quantitatively—increasingly important school catechesis",[6] the catechism became a textbook. This remained the principal aim until the publication in 1955 of the German Catechism, which was intended to be a family catechism, even though it never really succeeded in becoming one.

II. Catechisms as Testimonies to the Church's Faith

We have now reached the point where we can try to answer the question as to the real value of catechisms in obtaining a consensus of faith in the Church. In the first place, catechisms were produced, without any explicit commission on the part of the official Church, by individual believers—bishops, theologians or men active in pastoral work. Very many different authors could be named in this context.[7] Even though these authors were

---

[5] See J. Hofinger, "Katechismus", *op. cit.*, p. 46.
[6] J. Hofinger, *op. cit.*, p. 47.
[7] For the sixteenth century until the Counter-Reformation, see F. J. Kötter, *op. cit.*, pp. 24–111; for the period up to the middle of the nineteenth

writing in accordance with the universal faith of the Church and very often sought official recognition, their catechisms were, of course, also testimonies to their own personal faith. It is therefore correct, I think, to regard them as reflections of the faith of the Christian people made explicit by individual members of the Church. These catechisms therefore provide us with a genuine criterion for obtaining a consensus of faith at the level of the people of God.

On the other hand, however, many catechisms containing the obligatory teaching of the official Church were produced, especially at the time of the Reformation, with the authority of provincial and other councils[8]—the *Catechismus Romanus*, for example, being an authoritative document resulting from the Council of Trent.[9] These catechisms can be regarded as providing teaching about faith at the upper level in the Church, but we should not forget that they too were the work of individuals, in this case usually several outstanding theologians working together, with the result that they are also very important documents in obtaining a consensus of faith in the Church. The German catechism of 1955 was clearly a new type of catechism, even with regard to the way in which it came about.[10]

Seen from the point of view of their origin and development, then, catechisms can certainly be regarded as a real criterion for the faith of the Christian people and are as such very valuable in obtaining a consensus of faith in the Church. It is, of course, necessary to differentiate in individual cases and to give a higher rank to the official catechisms. The degree of universal recognition which a catechism by an individual author has received and

---

century, see F. X. Thalhofer, *Entwicklung des katholischen Katechismus in Deutschland von Canisius bis Deharbe* (Freiburg, 1899), pp. 1–121. See also J. Hofinger, *Geschichte des Katechismus in Österreich von Canisius bis zur Gegenwart* (Innsbruck and Leipzig, 1937), pp. 279–315.

[8] The provincial councils of Cologne (1536), Trier (1549), Mainz (1549) and Petrikau (1551) should be mentioned in this context.

[9] See G. Bellinger, *Der Catechismus Romanus und die Reformation. Die katechetische Antwort des Trienter Konzils auf die Haupt-Katechismen der Reformatoren* (Paderborn, 1970).

[10] See H. Fischer, "Zur Geschichte des neuen Katechismus", in *ibid.*, *Einführung in den neuen Katechismus* (Freiburg, 1955), pp. 1–6.

the extent to which it has been accepted provide a further criterion. Other aspects which need to be investigated are the degree to which it may have been subjected to distortion or stricture, and the materials and sources that have been used in its compilation.

III. The Effect of Catechisms on the Consciousness of Faith

If the value of catechisms in obtaining a consensus of faith is considered in terms of their effects, then we are bound to ask whether they have been of importance in stimulating knowledge and consciousness of faith. This question can be answered quite simply and directly. These catechisms have, since their first appearance, had a very lasting and deep influence on the faith and the consciousness of faith of Catholics—the same kind of effect that manuals of dogmatic theology have had on theological students.

A distinction ought perhaps to be made here between catechisms addressed to the whole community of believers (this is, of course, the real aim of catechesis[11]) and, since the transference of catechesis to the sphere of schools, those primarily intended for school use. I believe, however, that this distinction is of little importance now, because far greater stress has been placed, at least since the middle of the nineteenth century and the time of J. Deharbe, on correctness and completeness in, and the systematic presentation of, dogma. Taken as a whole, then, catechisms of all kinds have had a very pronounced and enduring effect on the conscious faith of German-speaking Catholics, far greater than the influence of Scripture or of the bishops' pastoral letters. The effects of these catechisms can be compared only with those of sermons; indeed, they may have had an influence greater than that of preaching in the course of the last hundred years. Hence, in their effects too, catechisms are very valuable in obtaining a consensus of faith in the German-speaking world.

[11] This important question has been dealt with by G. Biemer, *Handbuch der Verkündigung*, Vol. I (Freiburg, 1970), pp. 323–5; R. Padberg, *Handbuch der Pastoraltheologie*, Vol. I (Freiburg, ²1970), pp. 294–317; A. Exeler, *Wesen und Aufgabe der Katechese* (Freiburg, 1966), especially pp. 277–82.

Translated by David Smith

Jean Claude Dhôtel

French Catechisms and Consensus of Faith

DURING the eighteenth century the bishops took over the supervision of the editing and distribution of catechisms in France. The first catechisms, which appeared in the second half of the sixteenth century, were compiled by individuals, or by religious orders and communities of priests.[1] Some bishops adopted certain of these works before the appearance of the formula which was to become usual after 1660: "This catechism has been prepared at the order of Mgr... as the only one to be taught in his diocese."

Do these catechisms and the episcopal instructions which accompanied them tell us anything about the existence of a consensus of faith in France? In order to answer this question, it is necessary to ask two more:

1. What motives were behind the bishops' move to impose catechetical uniformity in their dioceses?

2. How is the problem of a consensus of faith posed in their catechisms?

First of all, one fact is irrefragable. Although catechesis was always practised in France, with more or less success and application, the catechism (in the sense of a short question-and-answer book mainly intended for the use of children) was a product of the Reformation. Calvin's was the first French catechism (1541). The first Catholic equivalent, P. Auger's catechism of 1563, was

---

[1] On the first French catechisms, see J. C. Dhôtel, *Les origines du catéchisme moderne* (Paris, 1967).

an almost word-for-word rejoinder. This similarity seemed suspect: "At the start of Calvin's schism", wrote a Jesuit of the period, "some persons decried the catechizing of the young and the use of the term 'catechism', all the more—so they said—because this was aping the Huguenots."[2] This reticence (as much as negligence) perhaps explains why, apart from notable exceptions, the bishops were slow in putting the Tridentine decisions into practice.

Once the anguish of the Religious Wars was over, the great Catholic reformers of the Church of France made the catechism one of their major concerns: whether in the towns (at the instigation, for example, of Olier or Bourdoise) or in the country (through the missions, and at the prompting of such men as Vincent de Paul, Jean Eudes or Julien Maunoir—all compilers of catechisms much renowned in the first half of the seventeenth century). Their intention was not, so it would seem, to restore the faith to a people that had supposedly lost it, but to combat "their extreme ignorance". "That", wrote one of them, "is the cause of the atrocious misfortune of so many Christians who hardly know what it means to be a Christian, who are Christian only in title, who enter our churches and come to the sacraments at Easter only because that was the custom of their fathers and forefathers, and who carry out all these practices without any awareness of what they are doing."[3] Beyond the statutory authorities of the episcopate and the university, these men intended to use the catechism as a means of unifying religious *knowledge*. The most remarkable initiative was certainly that of the Community of the Priests of St-Nicolas-du-Chardonnet, in Paris. The *curé*, Adrien Bourdoise, established something very much deserving of the title of an institute of pastoral catechetics, a centre for training and practical application—by way of his parish school.

The first diocesan catechism appeared in 1659 as the quite natural effect of a process which included a number of short works intended for priests, catechists, adults and children. In 1665, Archbishop Hardoin of Péréfixe sent it out with a pastoral injunction which contains the following statement: "Because it

[2] *Op. cit.*, p. 31.
[3] H. M. Boudon, *La Science sacrée du Catéchisme, op. cit.*, pp. 156–9.

is our duty to prevent the adversary from sowing tares among the wheat and corrupting purity of faith by false doctrines, we forbid you to teach or to cause to be taught to your pupils any catechism other than this. . . . We require this catechism to be read and taught in all the churches, colleges, schools and other places in which young people receive instruction."[4]

As in the previous century, it was a question of preserving the young from erroneous doctrine. Admittedly, Protestant writings were still in clandestine circulation, together—already—with some Jansenist tracts.[5] But one might justifiably ask whether this desire for uniformity did not have some additional grounds. There is, in fact, some evidence to show that it was just as much a question of re-establishing control over the religious institutes, which had been the primary instigators of the Catholic reformation. For example, there is the following severe notice from the Paris Chapter, addressed in 1678 to the Ursulines, who for almost a century had done sterling work among the people: "The superiors of the Ursulines have no special right in regard to the conduct of girls who are not members of the Order. This right belongs to the Paris Chapter, to which reference is to be made in regard to the catechisms and books used to teach these girls."[6]

Pastoral suasions also encouraged the tendency to uniformity. The care of "migrants" sometimes brought about the adoption of a metropolitan catechism or caused several bishops to agree on the composition of a single catechism for use in their dioceses. There is, for example, the catechism of the "three Henrys", who characterize their intention thus: "Since the proximity of our dioceses of Angers, La Rochelle and Luçon enable those within these dioceses to pass with ease from one to the other, we considered it appropriate to give them the one catechism, so that those who already are in close communication in matters of civil life should also have a special connection with one another in

---

[4] *Instruction de la Doctrine chrétienne ou Catéchisme fait par commandement de Mgr Hardoin de Péréfixe, archevêque de Paris* (Paris, 1665).

[5] For example, Saint-Cyran, *Théologie Familière* (Paris, 1639); M. Feydeau, *Catéchisme de la Grâce* (Paris, 1650).

[6] C. Joly, *Traité historique des écoles épiscopales et ecclésiastiques* (Paris, 1678), p. 428.

those pertaining to the Christian life."[7] In actuality, this publication did not help to obtain a consensus, for the catechism of the "three Henrys" is a typically Jansenist product.

In fact, notwithstanding declared intentions, uniformity remained quite relative. In 1687, Péréfixe's successor in Paris was astonished at the variety of catechisms published in his diocese; to redress the situation he imposed a new one. Sometimes a bishop—with or without grounds—would transfer to his new diocese the catechism in use in his old see.

In consideration of these difficulties, it seemed right to think of a single catechism for the Church of France. This measure, enforced by Napoleon, proved unsuccessful. Even though he chose the most famous (Bossuet's) nothing prevented a return to the old fragmentary approach once the Empire had collapsed. One bishop confirmed this setback: "It was not that we were not aware of the advantages which would result from having a general catechism for the whole of France and for the whole Church; but experience has taught us that a design which seems so simple is more difficult actually to carry out than could ever have been imagined. If the great Bossuet, who was so often the oracle of the Gallican Church, was unable to get all the suffragans to agree to his catechism, how could anyone be sure that any successor would achieve a more fortunate outcome?"[8] In fact, the second attempt (in 1937) was hardly less transient, for the *Catéchisme à l'usage des diocèses de France* hardly survived World War II.

In reality, the differences from one diocese to another were minimal in view of the sober uniformity of catechisms from the eighteenth century on. Even if they offer no evidence of the existence of a consensus of faith, they confirm that of a consensus of knowledge of the faith. But does the very idea of a consensus coincide with doctrinal content? This is the point we have to consider now, starting from the two characteristic attributes of the origin of catechisms, which—in a more or less pronounced form—were maintained subsequently: religious individualism and the spirit of controversy.

[7] *Catéchisme ou Doctrine chrétienne imprimé par ordre de Messeigneurs les Evêques d'Angers, de La Rochelle et de Luçon* (Paris, 1690).
[8] *Catéchisme du Diocèse de Valence* (Valence, 1814).

As soon as each Christian in schools, families, parishes and—
sometimes—missions was given the one *book*, a new relation was
set up between the faithful and the content of their faith.
Changing from its original condition of a rather diffuse feeling,
expressed mainly in collective phenomena, this content of faith
came to be a body of doctrine, a collection of truths summarized
in the symbol of the Apostles. It was presented as "that which
must be believed"—the rest of the catechism containing "that
which must be done"—in order to be saved, and not as that which
saves. Throughout the various definitions of faith, which remained astonishing stable for four centuries, there is an evident
and increasingly pronounced tendency to present a salvation
which everyone has to cling to rather as a shipwrecked sailor is
compelled to cling to his proverbial plank.

Admittedly there is also evident the notion of "profession of
faith", which implies communication, collective expression, and
consensus. Calvin in Geneva had instituted a ceremony for the
profession of faith: "When a child is sufficiently instructed to be
able to dispense with his catechism, let him recite solemnly all
that is contained therein, making in this way a profession of his
Christian faith in the presence of the Church."[9] This institution
was to be adopted much later by the Catholics. Of course it was
not really necessary: there are frequent acknowledgments that
the recitation of the Creed, or even of the Amen, at Sunday
Masses, as well as the sign of the cross, are professions of faith;
and that, above all, the sacrament of Confirmation is tantamount
to a *"Redditio Symboli"*. But, apart from the fact that it was administered to children of seven, various testimonies underline
the fact that it was very much neglected in France in the seventeenth and eighteenth centuries. For this reason, the solemn ceremony of "first communion" for children of twelve to fourteen
was invented (probably in the community of St-Nicolas-du-
Chardonnet. At the end of the seventeenth century, this ceremony was accompanied by that of the renewal of baptismal
promises, which came into general use. But the pastoral intention is clear: this ceremony was designed not so much as an expression of a consensus of faith as a public commitment of
children upon entry into a decisive period of their lives. The

[9] *Op. cit.*, p. 40.

second characteristic which escapes the notion of consensus is the spirit of controversy by which the catechisms were still marked. Consequently, except in regard to the article on the "communion of saints", the dogmatic content of which remained imprecise and varied from catechism to catechism, the solidarity of those who professed the same faith was conceived unanimously as the bond joining them individually to the Sovereign Pontiff, and was directed against errors and heretics. The emphasis placed on Romanism minimized the role of the bishops. Later, when controversy was dying down, there was an insistence on the parish, whose priest—formerly despised—became the "spiritual father", who saw himself as the absolute authority of the Pope over the universal Church on a local scale. As for the Church, it was defined more by its distinctive "marks" than by the inward unity of the same profession of faith.

Further development did not change this presentation, and the content of catechisms remained practically inviolable. Those of the eighteenth century were as unaffected by the philosophical movement as those of the first half of the nineteenth century. However, the Church's opponents were no longer so much the Protestants as the rationalists. But it was not until 1852, in a Paris catechism, that a few elements of rational theology were introduced: this was the first occasion on which there was any talk of "consensus"—but as a "proof" of the existence of God. Much later still, at the beginning of the nineteenth century, the adversary became the atheist pure and simple, which justified the introduction of a new approach: the starting-point was the religious fact, whose universality was affirmed before going on to revealed religion. If, therefore, there is any question of consensus (at a very late date) in catechisms, it is not one relating to what is specific to the Catholic faith.

To be sure, even though the catechisms and pastoral injunctions furnish much information on the practice of religion and behaviour, they are not much use when one is seeking to establish the existence of a consensus of faith. At the start, when it was a question of defence against the Reformation, there was an increasing flood of controversial catechisms in the areas most affected—but these matters are known from other sources. As for the Jansenist ideas of the following century, they were to some

extent diffused everywhere, but above all where they were pro-
moted by bishops. Superstitions were denounced, but, again,
they are to be found in the context of religious practice. In fact,
the catechisms and pastoral injunctions say nothing in regard to
the era when the unity of faith of the French people was threatened and broken. Once the great period of discovery between
about 1550 and 1660 was over, and in face first of all of the tidal
wave of Protestantism, and then in the course of the immense
task of rechristianizing France, the catechisms merely repeated
themselves, and remained outside the movement of secular ideas
—to such an extent that they wholly ignored the upheaval of the
French Revolution, as if it has been no more than a parenthesis
in French life between Louis XVI and the Restoration.

Translated by John Griffiths

PART III
DOCUMENTATION
CONCILIUM

Frans Haarsma

A Critical Community in Beverwijk

I. Origin

BEVERWIJK is a little town of about 40,000 inhabitants, not far from Amsterdam and Haarlem in the industrial district at the mouth of the river Ij. The ports, blast furnaces and paper mills draw workers from other parts of the Netherlands and from abroad. About 50% of the population is Catholic, 20% Protestant and the remaining 30% without specific church membership. Social and economic development is proceeding at a rapid rate.

The origin of the "critical community" of Beverwijk is to be found in the "beat Masses" organized in 1966 by an assistant priest, Jan Ruyter, in the parish of St Joseph, where the simple texts and the rhythmical singing supported by a children's choir and a band attracted great interest and became accepted as a new, beneficial experience of the liturgy. Until June 1970, the emphasis was still on the liturgy, which was extensively developed in those years. The choir was enlarged and its standard was raised. At the same time, the members of the parish were encouraged to participate actively, not only in the services, but in the preparation of texts, music, and so on. Even more important, themes such as the generation problem, peace, Biafra, the mentally sick and so on entered the liturgy, and writers and others who could help to work out themes were invited to take part. An inquiry yielded interesting results—for example, that younger people were participating less, and that 60% of those who came to the services were not members of the parish.

In 1968, the Septuagint group of contesting priests was formed and, since Jan Ruyter was one of the founder members, the aims of the movement were echoed at Beverwijk. From September 1969, themes such as priestly celibacy, intercommunion, and faith and politics, which were being urgently discussed in the Dutch Church, were chosen with increasing frequency at Beverwijk. But the people of Beverwijk soon realized that their debate, criticism and protest had to be extended beyond the walls of their church.

This conviction led to the second phase in the development of the parish, which began in June 1970, when the thematic celebrations of the liturgy grew into a "critical community". The first invitation to take part in *action groups*, ready to work locally wherever the need arose, resulted in more than a hundred volunteers. The services continued, but their purpose was now to inspire these groups to action outside the church. The groups, for example, visited local hospitals, helped old and lonely people and handicapped children, and made contact with foreign workers and the police and medical experts in connection with the drug problem. They also co-operated with existing bodies in the cause of peace and justice, often inviting these bodies to use their services as a platform.

Because so many of those who take part in the services come from elsewhere, these action groups are not confined to the parish of St Joseph, but are interconfessional. They are also independent, although a central secretariat is kept informed of what is going on in the groups. A "plenary assembly", composed mostly of representatives from all the action groups, meets every few months and discusses matters of concern to all the groups. There are also about thirty members of this "assembly" who are not members of action groups, but who are interested in the work of the critical community. Finally, each group is careful not to stand in the way of initiatives taken by other groups, but to do everything possible to support them.

II. Free Framework

It is hardly surprising that the services and the actions of this church in Beverwijk have encountered opposition, especially from the parishioners to whom the services have made no appeal.

The parish priest has a good relationship with his assistant, Jan Ruyter, but only partly agrees with his theological and liturgical views. He is consequently subject to pressure from the parishioners who object to Ruyter's work. This has led to an unsatisfactory situation in Beverwijk. The critical community feels that being bound to the parish (a bond which is visibly expressed in the position of the leader of the community as assistant parish priest, to the diocese of Haarlem, which seemed at most to tolerate the work of the community and to Rome and the other Catholic episcopal conferences, where the Dutch Church as a whole seems to stand alone in its search for a pastoral policy) is only an obstacle to free growth. The parish priest himself is also in a difficult situation as the leader of a divided parish, in which things happen which he can only partly support, but which he does not want to see disappear completely because they act as Christian leaven in the parish and far beyond its frontiers.

For these reasons, a declaration was made on 10 January 1971 by the community at Beverwijk, criticizing all the bodies mentioned above quite sharply and saying that the time had come for it to exist independently within a "free framework". Its members want to be free to find their own way, together with other local communities, without being rapped over the knuckles by the parish priest (who can hardly be expected to do anything else in the present circumstances) every time they act boldly. It is worth while quoting parts of this declaration here:

"We want to be a group trying to achieve today something that may be possible tomorrow on a greater scale. We want to be a community, a place where we are given the task of standing up for justice in the world, where critical questions are asked, where we are called upon to persist in our resistance to the machinery of prosperity and bureaucracy, and to the manipulation that degrades people. We want to be a place of meeting where we try again and again to understand the person and the words of Jesus of Nazareth. He has lit the flame of faith in us. He is our example. We want to follow him and look for the Father whose house has many rooms." After this manifesto, there is the emphatic statement: "We leave the traditional, time-honoured law to those who are convinced that it is right, but we know that we have to feel our way ahead and try out new paths "

The declaration of aims itself says: "We need this freedom because we know that the Church must now be able to provide a platform for all kinds of groups and actions. We want to carry out a programme in which many different alternatives can be accommodated in our church community. Too many sincere attempts to humanize the world are blocked as soon as they are confronted with human society. Together with others, we want to go further in experimentation. We want to put an end to the saying 'it just won't work'. We foresee that this free framework will radically change the nature and the form of our meetings. We will accept full responsibility for the risks and the consequences together with all the others who have consciously chosen our way."

The declaration closes with a question: "Can we continue our work in this church, independently and under our own responsibility, in contact with other local communities of a like mind and, as far as we are concerned, in constant dialogue with and inspired by the guidance of the church in Haarlem? We wait for a rapid, clear and relevant answer. If we feel that our demands are not taken seriously, we, the undersigned, are bound to say that we shall find it difficult to continue our activities."

III. In Search of a New Form of Community

In an attempt to find an answer to this question, a series of discussions was held at the beginning of 1971. Those taking part were the vicar-general of the Bishop of Haarlem, Mgr Kuipers, the parish priest of St Joseph's, Fr Pronk, his curate, Fr Ruyter, and several members of the action groups. These were later joined by representatives of three other similar groups and by a pastoral psychologist, W. Berger, and a pastoral theologian, F. Haarsma, both members of the department of pastoral theology of the theological faculty at Nijmegen. The Amsterdam pastoral theologian, B. Peters, guided the discussions.

In the first place, many underlying emotions, such as aggression, frustration, fear, and so on, were brought to the surface and canalized during the discussions, so that the way was cleared for a committed though objective approach to the problems. All concerned soon became aware of the existence of a number of aspects relating directly to the *Church* in the life and activities of the critical community in Beverwijk, aspects which were both legitimate and also hopeful signs for the future. The first of these was that the action groups experienced the Church as an *event*, not as an institution to which you belong whatever you do or do not do. The members of these action groups feel themselves to be a church only when they are closely united in preparing the service of the Word and the Eucharist, in celebrating it and in drawing its consequences. Their aim is to make a church at rest become a church in action, to make a church as a state of life into a church as an action in life. They see the Church more as the people of God passing through the desert than as the holy city and the temple on Mount Zion. They are more inspired by Paul, who, in Acts, goes out into the world, than by Peter, John and James, who are called the pillars of the Church in Jerusalem.

Very closely connected with this experience of the Church as an event is the experience of the Church as a *communio* or lived community. This is also an emotional experience. If the Church is not present as a lived and living community, the believer is conscious of a painful and guilty void. It is both a gift and a task, a risky undertaking.

Christians have often asked whether the fruit of the Spirit— love, joy, peace, patience, kindness, goodness, faithfulness, gentle- ness, self-control (Gal. 5. 22)—ought not to be consciously ex- perienced in some way. I have the impression that some of the fruit of the Spirit is sometimes experienced in these action groups. Just as the "works of the flesh"—immorality, impurity, licen- tiousness, idolatry, sorcery, enmity, strife, jealousy, anger, selfish- ness, dissension, party spirit, envy, drunkenness, carousing and the like (Gal. 5. 19–21)—form a negative criterion, so too does the fruit of the Spirit provide us with a positive criterion by which we can judge whether or not the Church is a true com- munity of Christ.

A third characteristic of these critical communities is their *charismatic structure*. An appeal is made to all members to place their talents at the disposal of the community and no one is excluded from the co-responsibility of the group as a whole. The priest or leader does not take over all the responsibility of all the members, nor does he try to do everything unaided—he places himself at their service as an expert, stimulates them to action and co-ordinates and integrates their activities. This is very clearly expressed in the fact that all take part in preparing and in celebrating the liturgical services, that all are involved in proclaiming God's word and in thinking and talking about it, and above all that everyone plays a part in the active service of their fellow men outside the walls of the church. Here, the specialized knowledge of the office-bearer may often be less than that of the lay people, with the result that there is little possibility of clericalism re-emerging in a cryptic form in these activities.

Not all, but very many of these communities have a *prophetic and critical attitude* towards the *status quo* in the Church and in society as a whole. This is sometimes expressed in demonstrations and protests, but quite often simply in making other people aware of injustice, oppression and discrimination, the symptoms of which are so commonly taken as a matter of course, and doing this in a less spectacular way. The members of these groups are mindful of the coming kingdom of God, with its promise of freedom, justice and peace, and oppose everything that contradicts these principles. They are convinced that the Christian community above all must not accept (in a spirit of resignation) injustice and the suppression of freedom by Church and society.

These groups are thus characterized, often more than the official churches, by an *eschatological dimension* of the kind that distinguished the first Christian communities, which were, after all, dominated by an expectation of the second coming of Christ and the kingdom of God. As Paul said: "The appointed time has grown very short; from now on, let those who have wives live as though they had none . . . and those who deal with the world as though they had no dealings with it. For the form of this world is passing away" (1 Cor. 7. 29–31). They seem to want to re-create the original meaning of the word "parish", that the members of the Christian community are "aliens and exiles" on the way to the promised land (1 Pet. 1. 1; 2. 11).

A further characteristic of these groups is that they place great emphasis on *serving their fellow men*, in contrast to the negative attitude of isolation from the world in the first Christian communities. This is the counterpart to their criticism of society, and accounts for their intense activity at the political level, both nationally and internationally. We are, of course, bound to ask questions about the possible futility of this activity and about the value or legitimacy of bringing concrete political action into worship, but there can be no doubt that this is inspired by a pure Christian motive—that of service.

The task of the Church in working for peace in the world and for better social, economic and political conditions today is discussed at length in the Pastoral Constitution *Gaudium et Spes* and the members of these action groups are quite right in their conviction that it is the local Christian communities, rather than "the Church", which have to carry out these tasks in the modern world. In obedience to the Gospel, they know that they must be a "Church for others" by serving their fellow men.

They go even further than this in the belief that the Church can only serve others fully by doing this *together with others*—in other words, both with non-Catholic Christians and with non-Christians who are prepared to support the same basic human values. In this way, one of the harmful side-effects of the charitable work that the churches have done for centuries is eliminated. This is the frequent confusion of motives—those of Christian love and of power.

Co-operation between Christians and all men of good will is an idea that was especially dear to the heart of John XXIII. It also inspires Paul VI in his work for peace and justice in the world. The Decree on Ecumenism calls co-operation a living expression of the bond that already binds all Christians together and one of the most important ways towards full unity. It must above all be put into practice in countries where social and technical development is taking place. We know more clearly now, however, than we did in 1964 that this includes the whole of the world. What the action groups are doing is very similar to what the decree suggests in paragraph 12—for example, working for peace and the dignity of man, applying the message of the Gospel to society, and helping men in their need.

Agreement was more difficult to reach during the discussions with regard to the form in which *unity* between these action groups and the Catholic Church should be expressed. Two concepts in particular which the Beverwijk community used in its declaration were discussed at length, but it proved impossible to define them clearly. These were the idea of the "free framework" and the term "under our own responsibility". It was, however, possible to clarify some aspects of these concepts.

In the first place, the critical community wanted to be free of the canonical laws governing the relationship between the parish priest and his curate and parishioners. The members of the community were looking for a form of unity in which the bond with the parish would not impede their free development as a community, but they did not want to relinquish that bond entirely, because that would entail a danger of mental isolation from the rest of the local Christian community and a loss of their function as "leaven". They were, however, prepared to accept this as the price that had to be paid for being Christians in the world without any compromise. External, administrative and static unity was less important to them than unity of inspiration and action. The second can, they believed, be made difficult or even impossible by the first.

The two debated terms, then, do not mean that these Christians refuse to give form to the bond binding them to other Christians or rather to the Church of Christ elsewhere. It is clear from their declaration that they want to continue their work "in contact with other local communities of a like mind and ... in constant dialogue with and inspired by the guidance of the church in Haarlem". They look to other, like-minded communities for encouragement, inspiration, criticism and correction. One suggestion made was that there should be a regular meeting of representatives from different critical communities at which each would justify the policy and activities of his community and let this be criticized by others, with the bishop or vicar-general playing an essential part in the discussion, not as a legal authority, but as a "defenceless" witness of the Christian tradition.

What the members of this critical community at Beverwijk were seeking, then, was not to be reintegrated into the existing church order, but rather the creation of sufficient latitude and freedom for new forms of being the Church to be developed. Very fortunately, the canons in the Codex relating to guilds, societies and confraternities which exist for the purpose of charitable works and/or public worship (*Codex Iuris Canonici*, cc. 707 ff.: *piae uniones, confraternitates*) were found to provide a possible opening. Such confraternities can receive the bishop's approval and they can even be formally established by him. The moderator has to be nominated by the bishop. They can be set up in a church or in a public oratory. If they have no church, they can hold their exercises in the chapel or at the altar of the church in which they have been established, on the understanding that the parish services do not suffer in any way. Finally, the property and money of these confraternities must be kept separate from the possessions of the parish church.

On the basis of this discovery, the diocese of Haarlem designed a fairly flexible juridical structure, within which the critical community of Beverwijk would be able to use the parish church of St Joseph for certain services. The community will not be directly accountable to the parish priest for its activities, nor will it be financially dependent on the parish council. Ultimately, however, the parish would continue to be the framework within which the critical community would operate, so that a certain ambivalence still persists.

It is clear, then, that an attempt has been made here to preserve something valuable that has already developed and to give it the opportunity to develop further, while avoiding a breach with the diocese and the parish that could result in sectarianism. Only the future can show us whether it will be possible for the critical community of Beverwijk to continue along this path. If both sides have the courage to experiment, it should be possible·

Translated by David Smith

Note.—A documentary account of the critical community and its development has recently been published: Jan Ruyter and Richard Anwerda, *Welkom en ongewenst. 5 jaar zoeken in Beverwijk* (Hilversum, 1971).

Biographical Notes

NORBERT BROX was born 23 June 1935 in Paderborn and is a Catholic. Doctor of theology and qualified in patrology and ecumenism, he is professor of Catholic theology and of religious pedagogy at the University of Munich, and assistant professor of patrology at the University of Regensburg. Among his published works are: *Offenbarung, Gnosis und gnostischer Mythos bei Irenäus von Lyon* (Salzburg/Munich, 1966) and *Paulus und Seine Verkündigung* (Munich, 1966).

ADALBERT DAVIDS was born in 1937 in The Netherlands. He studied philosophy, theology, byzantinology and Eastern and Slavonic languages at Louvain, Rome, Salzburg and Munich. Doctor of theology, he is lecturer on patrology and on ancient history of the Church at the University of Nijmegen. He is the author of many articles on Greek, Syrian and Slavonic ascetical and mystical literature.

JEAN CLAUDE DHÔTEL, S.J., was born 30 September 1926 in Paris and was ordained in 1958. After studying at the Faculty of Theology of Lyons-Fourvière, he received the degree of doctor from the Faculty of Theology of Paris for a thesis on the origins of the Catechism in France. He is corresponding editor of the review *Vie Chrétienne*.

MGR ANTONIO FRAGOZO was born 10 December 1920 at Teixeira (Brazil). He studied at the Major Seminary of Pessoa. Ordained priest in 1944, he was consecrated auxiliary bishop of São Luis in 1957 and nominated first residential bishop of Crateús in 1964. He took part in four sessions of Vatican II.

FRANS HAARSMA was born 19 July 1921 in Balk (Netherlands) and ordained in 1947. He studied at the University of Nijmegen. Doctor of theology, he is professor of pastoral theology at the University of Nijmegen. Among his published works is *Geest en Kirk. Een pastoraal-oecumenische studie over de ecclesiologi van Dr. O. Noordmans* (1967).

Ruud Huysmans was born in 1935 in Eindhoven and ordained in 1959. He studied at the Lateran University, Rome. Doctor of laws and of canon law, he is lecturer on canon law at the High School of Catholic Theology in Amsterdam and a member of the managing committee of the Pastoral Institute of the ecclesiastical province of The Netherlands. Among his published works are articles on impediments to mixed marriages in *Ephemerides Iuris Canonici* in 1967 and 1969.

Franz Joseph Kötter was born in 1928 in Löningen (Germany) and ordained in 1954. He studied in Münster and Rome. Doctor of theology, he is professor of Catholic religious pedagogy at the High School of Pedagogy in Niedersachsen. Among his published works is *Die Eucharistielehre in den katholischen Katechismen des 16. Jahrhunderts bis zum Erscheinen des Catechismus Romanus* (1566) (Münster, 1966).

Hervé-Marie Legrand, o.p., was born 5 October 1935 in France and ordained in 1963. He studied at the Faculties of the Saulchoir (France) and Walberberg (Germany) and at the Universities of St Thomas (Rome), Strasburg and Athens. Licentiate in philosophy, doctor of theology and a graduate in canon law, he is a professor at the Faculty of Theology of the Saulchoir. Among his publications are contributions to the collective works *La charge pastorale des évêques* (Unam Sanctam 74) (Paris, 1969) and *Pour une théologie du ministère* (Gembloux/Paris, 1971).

Leonardus Meulenberg was born in 1936 in Doenrade (Netherlands). He studied at Rolduc, at the Major Seminary of Roermond and at the Gregorian (Rome). Doctor of theology, he teaches Church history at the High School of Theology and the Pastorate in Heerlen. Among his published works are: *Der Primat der Römischen Kirche im Denken und Handeln Gregors VII* (The Hague, 1965) and "Enkele historische kanttekeningen bij de keuze van een bisschop", in *Theologie en Pastoraat*, no. 1 (1971).

Carlo Molari was born 25 July 1928 in Cesena (Italy) and ordained in 1952. He studied at the Lateran University. Doctor of theology and of civil and canon law, he is professor of dogmatic theology at the University "de propaganda fide" (Rome). Among his published works are: *De Christi ratione essendi et operandi* (Rome, 1958) and *Teologia e diritto canonico in S. Tommaso d'Aquino* (Rome, 1962).

Mgr Paul Moore was born in Morristown (U.S.A.) in 1919. He studied at Yale University. Doctor of theology (h.c.), he was consecrated coadjutor bishop of the Episcopalian diocese of New York in 1964. He is also a member of the Yale Corporation, trustee of the General Theological Seminary, and on the steering committee of the Association "Clergy and Laymen Concerned about Vietnam".

Alois Müller was born 20 September 1924 in Basle and was ordained in 1949. He studied at the University of Fribourg, at the Angelicum (Rome) and the Institut supérieur de catéchétique (Paris). Doctor of theology, he is professor of pastoral theology at the University of Fribourg. Among his published works are: *Das Problem von Befehl und Gehorsam im Leben der Kirche* (1964) and *Die neue Kirche und die Erziehung* (1966). The first of these books has been translated into English, and the second into English, French and Hungarian.

MGR LEONIDAS PROAÑO was born in 1910 in San Antonio de Ibarra (Ecuador). He studied at the Major Seminary of Quito. Ordained priest in 1936, he was consecrated Bishop of Riobamba in 1954. He is also president of the Evangelization and Education Commission of Ecuador.

MGR GEORG WAGNER was born in 1930 in a Protestant family and joined the Orthodox Church in 1948. He studied at the St Serge Institute of Orthodox Theology in Paris, and at the Faculty of Philosophy of the Free University of West Berlin. Doctor of philosophy, he is professor of canon law and of liturgical theology at the St Serge Institute. Ordained priest in 1955, he was consecrated titular bishop of Eudociade on 3 October 1971, having been chosen by the Synod of the Ecumenical Patriarchate of Constantinople. Among his published works is *Der Ursprung der Chrisostomos-liturgie.*